Praise for Immaculée's first book, *Left to Tell*

"I am humbled by the extraordinary spirituality that shines throughout Immaculée Ilibagiza's story of terror, endurance, healing, and forgiveness. As a Rwandan, I am proud that we can look beyond the misconceived differences that resulted in the murder of so many of our children, men, and women in 1994. Immaculée's account of genocide survival is truly astonishing. It gives us hope of overcoming the divisions deliberately created by those with self-serving agendas and no thought for humanity. Everyone should read this story—survivors as well as perpetrators. I hope that all can experience Immaculée's profound spiritual transformation and be inspired to work for a united and lasting nation."

— **Jeannette Kagame**, First Lady of the Republic of Rwanda

"In 1994, Rwandan native Ilibagiza was [24] years old and home from college to spend Easter with her devout Catholic family when the death of Rwanda's Hutu president sparked a three-month slaughter of [more than] one million ethnic Tutsis. She survived by hiding in a Hutu pastor's tiny bathroom with seven other starving women for 91 cramped, terrifying days. This searing firsthand account of Ilibagiza's experience cuts two ways: her description of the evil that was perpetrated, including the brutal murders of her family members, is soul-numbingly devastating, yet the story of her unquenchable faith and connection to God throughout the ordeal uplifts and inspires. This book is a precious addition to the literature that tries to make sense of humankind's seemingly bottomless depravity and counter-balancing hope in an all-powerful, loving God."

— ***Publishers Weekly***

"We all ask ourselves what we would do if faced with the kind of terror and loss that Immaculée Ilibagiza faced during the genocide in her country. Would we allow fear and desperation to fill us with hatred or despair? And should we survive, would our spirit be poisoned, or would we be able to rise from the ashes still encouraged to fulfill our purpose in life, still able to give and receive love? In the tradition of Viktor Frankl and Anne Frank, Immaculée is living proof that human beings can not only withstand evil, but can also find courage in crisis, and faith in the most hopeless of situations. She gives us the strength to find wisdom and grace during our own challenging times."

— **Elizabeth Lesser**, co-founder of the Omega Institute, and author of *Broken Open: How Difficult Times Can Help Us Grow*

LED BY FAITH

ALSO BY IMMACULÉE ILIBAGIZA, WITH STEVE ERWIN

LED BY FAITH: Rising from the Ashes of the Rwandan Genocide
(4-CD abridged audio book)

LEFT TO TELL: Discovering God Amidst the Rwandan Holocaust
(also available in Spanish and as a 4-CD abridged audio book)

*OUR LADY OF KIBEHO: Messages from the Mother of
God in the Heart of Africa* (available November 2008)

❖ ❖

HAY HOUSE TITLES OF RELATED INTEREST

YOU CAN HEAL YOUR LIFE, the movie, starring Louise L. Hay
& Friends (available as a 1-DVD program and an expanded 2-DVD set)
Watch the trailer at: **www.LouiseHayMovie.com**

❖ ❖

AN ATTITUDE OF GRATITUDE: 21 Life Lessons, by Keith D. Harrell

*CHANGE YOUR THOUGHTS—CHANGE YOUR LIFE:
Living the Wisdom of the Tao,* by Dr. Wayne W. Dyer

COUNT YOUR BLESSINGS: The Healing Power of Gratitude and Love,
by Dr. John F. Demartini

*IF I CAN FORGIVE, SO CAN YOU: My Autobiography
of How I Overcame My Past and Healed My Life,* by Denise Linn

*THE POWER OF INTENTION: Learn to Co-create Your World
Your Way,* by Dr. Wayne W. Dyer

PRACTICAL PRAYING: Using the Rosary to Enhance Your Life,
by John Edward (book-with-CD)

PRAYER AND THE FIVE STAGES OF HEALING,
by Ron Roth, Ph.D., with Peter Occhiogrosso

YOUR SOUL'S COMPASS: What Is Spiritual Guidance?
by Joan Z. Borysenko, Ph.D., and Gordon Franklin Dveirin, Ed.D.

❖ ❖

All of the above are available at your local bookstore,
or may be ordered by visiting:

Hay House USA: **www.hayhouse.com**®
Hay House Australia: **www.hayhouse.com.au**
Hay House UK: **www.hayhouse.co.uk**
Hay House South Africa: **www.hayhouse.co.za**
Hay House India: **www.hayhouse.co.in**

LED BY FAITH

Rising from the Ashes
of the Rwandan Genocide

IMMACULÉE
ILIBAGIZA

with Steve Erwin

HAY HOUSE, INC.
Carlsbad, California • New York City
London • Sydney • Johannesburg
Vancouver • Hong Kong • New Delhi

Published and distributed in the United States by: Hay House, Inc.: www.hayhouse.
com • *Published and distributed in Australia by:* Hay House Australia Pty. Ltd.: www.
hayhouse.com.au • *Published and distributed in the United Kingdom by:* Hay House
UK, Ltd.: www.hayhouse.co.uk • *Published and distributed in the Republic of South
Africa by:* Hay House SA (Pty), Ltd.: www.hayhouse.co.za • *Distributed in Canada by:*
Raincoast: www.raincoast.com • *Published in India by:* Hay House Publishers India:
www.hayhouse.co.in

Editorial supervision: Jill Kramer   •   *Design:* Tricia Breidenthal
Interior photos courtesy of the author

Library of Congress Cataloging-in-Publication Data

Ilibagiza, Immaculée.
  Led by faith : rising from the ashes of the Rwandan genocide / Immaculée Ilibagiza ;
with Steve Erwin. -- 1st ed.
    p. cm.
  ISBN 978-1-4019-1887-3 (hardcover : alk. paper) -- ISBN 978-1-4019-1888-0 (tradepa-
per : alk. paper) 1. Ilibagiza, Immaculée. 2. Rwanda--History--1994- 3. Rwanda--His-
tory--Civil War, 1994--Personal narratives. 4. Rwanda--History--Civil War, 1994--Refu-
gees. 5. Refugees--Rwanda--Biography. 6. Refugees--United States--Biography. 7.
Rwandans--United States--Biography. 8. Christian life--Catholic authors. I. Erwin,
Steve. II. Title.
  DT450.443.I44 2008
  282.092--dc22
  [B]   2008013364

Hardcover ISBN: 978-1-4019-1887-3
Tradepaper ISBN: 978-1-4019-1888-0

11 10 09 08   4 3 2 1
1st edition, September 2008

Printed in the United States of America

To Wayne Dyer . . .
for your kindness
and selfless friendship,
and for bringing my story
to the world with love

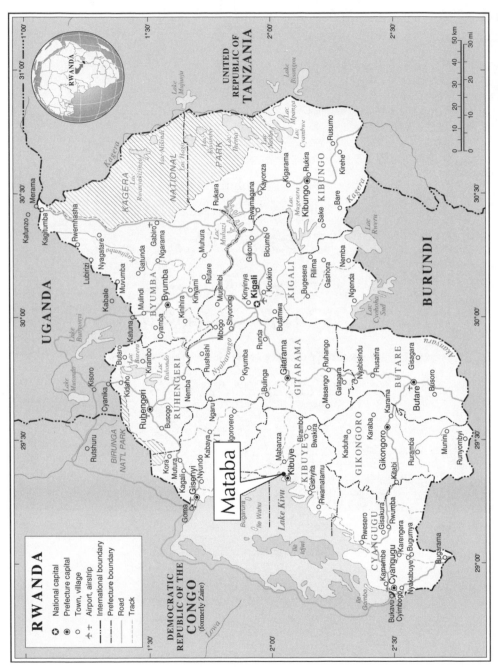

Mataba, Immaculée's home village, which is on the shores of Lake Kivu.

CONTENTS

"For truly, I say to you, if you have faith like a grain of mustard seed, you will say to this mountain, 'Move from here to there,' and it will move, and nothing will be impossible for you."

— MATTHEW 17:20

"Faith is the strength by which a shattered world shall emerge into the light."

— HELEN KELLER

PREFACE

As was the case with my first book, what I have written in these pages is not intended to be a history of Rwanda or of the genocide. I leave the detailed chronicling and political analysis of those 100 days of slaughter to the historians, journalists, professors, and politicians. For my part, I write about my own personal story—about surviving the genocide, yes, but also about finding a life worth living through faith and in the healing power of forgiveness. It is a true story; the events are real, and I use my own name and those of my family. However, I have changed the names and titles of some who appear in this book to protect the identity, privacy, and safety of the survivors.

— **Immaculée Ilibagiza**, New York City
Fall 2008

INTRODUCTION

Wake-Up Call

The screams woke me with a start.

Reaching into the darkness, I felt for Nikeisha (or Nikki), my beautiful baby girl. She'd been sick with a cold all day and night and hadn't slept for more than a few minutes. Neither had I. For the hundredth time that night, I yearned for my own mother.

Where are you, Mom? Oh, how I need your help! I have no one to teach me how to ease this child's pain, I thought, climbing out of bed and moving to Nikki's crib.

My mom had always been able to comfort my brothers and me when we were ill, hurt, or frightened. But she never got the chance to pass on those skills, or the myriad secrets of child rearing she'd learned from my grandmother, to me. The maternal line had been cut; my mother had been taken from me, along with all of her love and knowledge.

As I sat on the edge of the bed and cradled my little one in my arms, my heart ached. Nikki would never feel the loving touch of her nana's hand, nor would she hear the gentle voice of her grandpapa, who would surely have spoiled her rotten. As I recalled how much my mother had dreamed of having grandchildren, I wondered, *Mom, do you see her? Isn't your first grandchild precious?*

How many years would pass before my daughter asked me what had happened to her grandparents, why she'd never met the uncles she saw in the family photo album, and what it was like where Mommy grew up?

What would I say to her? How could I explain the story of Rwanda, of how the people I'd trusted all my life—neighbors, teachers, and friends—had turned into monsters more terrifying than any nightmare she would ever have? How many birthdays needed to go by before my child would be prepared to hear that her nana, grandpapa, and uncles were slaughtered along with more than a million other innocent Rwandans? That they'd been cut down for no other reason than being born Tutsi? What would be the appropriate age for her to learn about genocide?

What words could I find to describe to Nikki what had been done to my family? My pain was such that it still prevented me from sharing those horrible events with my only surviving brother, Aimable, even though years had passed and I'd moved far away to a new life in America.

Yet I knew it was a tale I had to share, one that I'd been left to tell. I believed that God had spared me during the genocide for a reason: to talk to as many people as I could about how He had touched my heart amidst the holocaust and taught me to forgive. I was to bear witness to how this one act can save a soul crippled by hatred and sickened by the desire for revenge.

I hoped that those who listened to my story would see that my shattered heart had been mended through forgiveness and ask, "If *her* heart can recover, why not mine?"

Why couldn't forgiveness heal a million broken hearts and revive a broken nation? The answer is that it can heal *all* hearts and nations. That was the story that needed to be told; that was my story.

NIKKI HAD STOPPED CRYING AND WAS NOW SLEEPING PEACEFULLY IN MY ARMS. I placed her back in the crib, kissed her on the forehead, and softly whispered in her ear, "I'm going to write a story for God, but it's also for you. When you grow up, you can read the story, and in its pages you'll meet your grandparents and uncles and learn how much they would have loved you."

My daughter had given me a wake-up call. It was the middle of the night, but I was no longer tired—my baby was breathing easily, and I had much to tell her and anyone else who would listen.

Sitting at my rickety computer table across the room from Nikki, I placed my fingers on the keyboard and prayed to my favorite saint, the Virgin Mary, to guide my words, and then I began. I typed through the night, and kept on typing every night, week after week, until I'd written "The End." My effort culminated in a massive stack of paper on the floor beside me, and I prayed that the Lord would let me know what to do with it because I didn't have a clue.

Of course, as He always does when we have even a speck of faith, God answered my prayer. It would take years—a few rewrites, visits from many guardian angels, and another beautiful baby—but God did answer my prayer, leading me to an "accidental" meeting with the inspiring writer and motivational speaker Wayne Dyer in 2004 at a conference on spirituality.

Wayne was signing copies of his new book, and when I approached him to have my copy signed, he began chatting with me in his friendly and inquisitive manner. Within a few minutes, this lovely man had me telling him about how God had touched my heart during the genocide and taught me to forgive my family's killers. Wayne listened . . . and then shocked me by promising to take my manuscript to his publisher and turn it into a book. He was good to his word, and before I knew it, *Left to Tell: Discovering God Amidst the Rwandan Holocaust* had been published and became an international bestseller.

Since that first book of mine came out in 2006, it has been translated into more than a dozen languages, from Icelandic to Japanese, and I've been invited to visit countries I'd never even heard of as a child in my little African village. What a glorious gift to meet so many new and wonderful people, share my story, and talk about faith and forgiveness! In fact, few things have given me more joy or a greater sense of purpose.

No matter where I go, others seem astonished that I've been able to forgive those who persecuted me and murdered my family. People often tell me that there is something different or remarkable about me, saying, "You're a saint for forgiving those killers the way you did. You truly are a saint." Of course I'm not a saint.

Nor is there anything remarkable about me—I still struggle with pain, fear, and anger like every other human does. But whenever those feelings surface, I remember how God saved me and gave me strength. The Lord is always there for me, just as He is for any of us in our time of need. But we must always be ready to receive Him into our hearts, and I hope *that* is what people can take away from my story.

I'VE WRITTEN THIS SECOND BOOK TO SHARE MORE OF MY STORY WITH YOU. Much of this was only touched upon in *Left to Tell,* so I wanted to flesh out what happened to me in the years after the genocide, when I had to fight to keep my relationship with God foremost in my heart. Yet I didn't write *Led by Faith* as a chronological, day-to-day diary about living in a postholocaust world. Instead, I wanted to share my saga of survival through a string of deeply personal experiences and memories connecting and highlighting the events that most profoundly influenced my spiritual growth.

Our national nightmare had rocked my country to its core; suffering, sorrow, mistrust, and fear were everywhere. Although I'd fully surrendered myself to God's will during the genocide—embracing His love and accepting Him as my heavenly Father, dearest friend, and protector—my life was now filled with new and terrifying challenges I never could have anticipated. In the dark and confusing world that unfolded around me, my struggle to find meaning, understanding, and hope continued.

It was through that struggle that I was taught one of the most important lessons I've ever learned: Never take faith for granted. Our relationship with the Lord is the most glorious love affair we will ever experience, but like all relationships, it demands nurturing—it requires hard work, constant attention, and deep commitment in order to grow stronger and flourish. The renewal of faith continues to take place in my life, and I have watched in wonder as the people of Rwanda renew their faith in God, and as the wounds of genocide are healed through His love.

Even in the best of times, life is challenging, and earthly concerns can too easily interfere with our spirituality. As I stumbled through the aftermath of the holocaust, I learned that finding the Lord is not enough; we have to *keep* Him in our heart always. We need to constantly discover God anew, trust Him in all things great and small, and make sure that He remains part of our daily life. We must always allow our hearts to be led by faith.

CHAPTER 1

LEFT TO TELL

For those of you who haven't read *Left to Tell* and are unfamiliar with me, let me introduce myself and briefly recap what I shared in my first book. (Those of you who have read that work may also appreciate this chance to brush up on my history.)

My name is Immaculée Ilibagiza. I was born in Rwanda, the tiny country in central Africa that most of the world knows about for one reason: the 1994 genocide in which more than a million innocent people were viciously slaughtered in the cruelest ways imaginable. Yet as a child, I couldn't have imagined a happier or more peaceful place to grow up.

Rwanda is one of the most physically beautiful places in the world, made up of endless rolling hills, pine and cedar forests, and lush green valleys. It is blessed with such a lovely, temperate climate throughout the year that the first European settlers named it "the land of eternal spring." I personally thought that I'd been born into paradise.

I grew up in a small village called Mataba, in the western province of Kibuye. My family's home sat atop a hill overlooking the vast and sparkling waters of Lake Kivu. Across the lake were breathtaking views of the snowcapped mountains in our

1

neighboring country of Zaire, now called the Democratic Republic of the Congo.

While Rwanda is roughly the size of the American state of Maryland, it has a population of more than eight million, making it one of the most densely populated countries in the world. It is also one of the poorest. Our rural village had a one-room schoolhouse and no running water or electricity. The people, however, seemed genuinely kind and friendly. Our neighbors were our extended family, their doors always open to us and ours to them. As a child, I never felt threatened by, or afraid of, anyone we knew.

My parents, Rose and Leonard, were warm and generous people who were adored by their four children: my two older brothers, Aimable and Damascene; my younger brother, Vianney; and me. Mom and Dad were the first in their families to graduate from high school, and among the few in the region ever to go to college. They both became teachers and believed that the only way to escape the poverty crippling so much of Africa was through a good education. They drilled us kids relentlessly after school on all of our subjects to ensure that our marks were among the highest in the province.

Many of the villagers or their children had been pupils of my parents, and Mom and Dad were so respected in our community that they were often called on for advice or to settle local disputes. I particularly remember how the men in the area would approach my father after church on Sundays with questions about which crops to plant, what they had to do to keep their children in school longer, or how much to pay for a neighbor's cow.

Church was a very big deal for us. In our house, God was loved and worshipped, and prayer was a daily ritual. Although my parents were devout Catholics, they believed that God was found in all faiths and religions, and they encouraged us to live by the Golden Rule—that is, to always treat our neighbors with love and respect.

My three brothers and I were very fond of each other, and we were happy to grow up together in Mataba. Since we didn't have any shopping malls, video games, television, or even telephones, we had to amuse ourselves. So when we weren't doing chores or homework, we spent most of our free time together playing games, swimming in Lake Kivu, or staying home and sharing stories with one another.

In almost every way, my childhood was idyllic. It wasn't until I was well into my schooling that I realized our parents had protected my brothers and me from the truth about Rwanda. We grew up believing that our neighbors loved and cared for us and that our country was safe and peaceful. We were never told about the ugly prejudices, simmering ethnic tensions, and hate-mongering politics that had been driving our compatriots apart, which ultimately laid the groundwork for one of history's bloodiest genocides.

BEFORE I ENTERED THE SCHOOL SYSTEM, I'd never heard of people being referred to as *Hutus* or *Tutsis,* but once enrolled, I couldn't escape the horrible shadow those words cast across Rwanda.

My education in the country's unique style of apartheid began when, as a young girl, I was forced to stand up in class in the mornings and identify myself as a member of the Tutsi tribe. Rwanda is home to the following tribes: the Hutu majority, which accounts for roughly 85 percent of the nation's inhabitants; and my tribe, the Tutsis, which make up about 14 percent. The other one percent of the population belongs to the Twa, a pygmy-like tribe who mostly live and hunt in the country's forests and keep to themselves.

Even though Hutus and Tutsis belonged to different tribes, we shared a single culture: we all spoke the same language (Kinyarwanda), ate the same foods, worshipped in the same churches, studied in the same classrooms, and lived in the same neighborhoods and even in the same homes. While Tutsis were supposed to be taller and have fairer skin and narrower noses than the Hutus, generations of intermarriage had essentially eradicated such differences. Hutu and Tutsi blood had mingled for so many centuries that, by the time I was born in 1970, the tribes were virtually indistinguishable. Politically, however, we had been kept apart with ruthless efficiency.

As is the case in much of Africa, many of Rwanda's modern problems were rooted in the colonial past.

For more than 500 years, Hutus and Tutsis had lived in peace under a long line of Tutsi kings. But that peace was shattered when European colonizers—first the Germans, and later the Belgians—arrived in Rwanda in the 19th century. To more easily conquer and control the country, the Belgians supported the Tutsi monarchy and exploited the existing social structure. The Belgians favored the Tutsis because their lighter skin and finer features made them seem more closely related to Europeans than the Hutus. The Belgian overlords even introduced an "ethnic identity card" to guarantee that the two groups remained as socially segregated as possible.

When the Tutsi king pressed for independence and asked the Belgians to leave Rwanda in 1959, the Belgians retaliated by helping Hutu extremists seize power and topple the centuries-old Tutsi monarchy. The bloody Hutu Revolution that followed left more than 100,000 Tutsis dead. After the Belgians pulled out of Rwanda in 1962, Hutu extremists began a decades-long campaign of terror and slaughter aimed at Tutsis. Tens of thousands of men, women, and children were murdered during the frequent anti-Tutsi pogroms and ethnic cleansings encouraged by the country's new rulers.

As soon as these extremists put policies in place to make sure that the best jobs and school placements now went to Hutus, Tutsi politicians were ousted from office, Tutsi professors were fired from their teaching jobs, and top Tutsi students were passed over for scholarships. The system of tribal identity cards was now used to isolate, intimidate, and persecute Tutsis. When hundreds of thousands of Tutsis fled Rwanda to escape the killing sprees, the Hutu government seized the opportunity to banish them permanently. As a result, generations of Tutsis lived in exile in the countries bordering Rwanda, forbidden by law to return to their homeland.

By the time I was a teenager in the 1980s, many of those exiled had joined a political movement in Uganda called the Rwandan Patriotic Front (RPF). The RPF demanded that the Hutu government stop persecuting Tutsis in Rwanda and allow the exiles to return home. The government, which became a virtual dictatorship after a 1973 coup by Juvénal Habyarimana, refused such demands, so rebel Tutsi soldiers invaded northern Rwanda from Uganda. The rebels said that they would fight until the Hutu government agreed to share power with them and treat Tutsis as equals.

The invasion triggered an on-again, off-again civil war that started when I was away at high school in the fall of 1990. Anti-Tutsi policies intensified during this time, reaching levels of hatred and intolerance not seen in the world since the Nazis' persecution of Jews decades before. One of the most blatant tools of hate came in the form of "the Hutu Ten Commandments," which first appeared in an anti-Tutsi newspaper. This piece of propaganda declared it an act of treason for a Hutu to marry, or even lend money or conduct business with, a Tutsi. Meaningful government or military jobs were barred to Tutsis at this point; and all Hutus were encouraged to shun their Tutsi neighbors, relatives, and friends.

A political movement called "Hutu Power" spread across the country, using "hate radio" on the government's own station to promote intense national fear and loathing of Tutsis. Hutu radio programs dehumanized Tutsis, labeling them as "cockroaches" that had to be "exterminated" before they could harm Hutu children or steal Hutu jobs. Such programs reached the entire country, and it became clear that the government was openly supporting a policy of mass murder to deal with "the Tutsi problem."

It was a frightening time that only became more unstable when the political party of President Juvénal Habyarimana began recruiting and training tens of thousands of unemployed young Hutu men into a paramilitary militia known as the *Interahamwe,* which means, literally, "those who kill together." Their sole mission was the extermination of the "Tutsi cockroaches."

By April 1994, the fuel for genocide had been gathered and prepared, and it was ready to be ignited. The spark was struck on Easter weekend, when I was home from university visiting my family for the holiday.

THE NIGHT BEFORE THE GENOCIDE BEGAN, my brother Damascene begged our family to leave the village with him immediately because he'd heard that groups of Interahamwe were wandering through our area armed with machetes and hand grenades. He also warned us that they were carrying a Tutsi death list.

"Our names are on that list," my brother said, pleading with my dad to get us out of the country that night. He promised us that he'd find a boat down the hill and row us across Lake Kivu to safety in Zaire.

But my father remained unconvinced. "You're too young to know what you're talking about," he told Damascene. "I've seen this kind of panic before . . . rumors start going around about death lists, and then everyone is suddenly seeing killers with grenades behind each bush."

Like me, Dad believed that our neighbors were good and kind people incapable of harming us. There were some political problems because of the war, but that didn't affect us—our village was one big happy family. Even my boyfriend, John, was a Hutu, and we planned to get married after university. So I agreed with my father and didn't think things were nearly as bad as Damascene was making them out to be.

"Besides, the Hutu president just signed a peace accord with the Tutsi rebels agreeing to share power and let the exiles back into Rwanda," Dad added. "Things haven't been looking this good for Tutsis in years. Leave it to your elders to decide what's what, Damascene. I'm not about to pack up my family and leave my home because some of your pals are making up stories."

But my brother was so passionate about what he was saying that he eventually convinced me he was right. I remembered the radio broadcasts calling for Hutus to exterminate the Tutsi cockroaches, and troubling anti-Tutsi demonstrations I'd seen in the streets near my university town.

"Maybe Damascene is right, Dad. Maybe we should leave now . . ."

Dad's response was to end our conversation abruptly.

"No one in this family is going anywhere," he said. "I am older and know better."

By the next morning, April 7, it didn't matter anymore whether Damascene had been right or wrong—it was too late for any of us to escape.

President Habyarimana had been killed when his plane was shot down during the night while returning from peace talks. Within the hour, Hutu extremists set their carefully laid plans for genocide in motion. The killing started immediately in Rwanda's capital, Kigali; any Tutsis or Hutu moderates who might have hindered the launch of the holocaust were dragged from their homes and executed in the streets with their families.

Death squads immediately sprang up in our village as well, and the slaughter of our Tutsi friends and neighbors began. The Interahamwe set homes on fire and hacked entire families to death with machetes as they tried to escape the flames. The screams echoed in the hills around Mataba, but there was nowhere to run. Escape routes out of the country, including by boat across Lake Kivu, had been cut off. Government soldiers and Interahamwe killers had set up roadblocks and checkpoints everywhere, and carrying a Tutsi identity card was a death sentence.

As the killers moved from hut to hut, hundreds of panicked villagers ran to our house looking to my father for help. My parents had been community leaders, and now the Tutsi community was depending on them to save their lives. Soon thousands of Tutsis from across the region were camped out in front of our home, waiting for my dad to tell them what to do.

For the next two days my father tried to calm the terrified crowd, urging them to defend themselves as best they could until help arrived. But so many were women and children, and the young men who were willing to fight had no weapons. Everyone was scared to death; I remember thinking that we were all sitting around like lambs waiting to be slaughtered.

On the third day, the attacks began. At first the men in the crowd held the Interahamwe back by throwing sticks and stones, but they kept coming in larger and larger groups, carrying machetes, spears, and clubs studded with nails.

Before the attacks became a massacre, my father instructed me to run to the home of a local Hutu pastor with my younger brother's friend Augustine.

"Get out of here now, Immaculée," my father ordered. "Pastor Murinzi is a good man and a good friend. Ask him to hide you until all this trouble is settled."

I begged him to let me stay—I worried I'd never see him or my mother or brothers again. But he insisted I leave, saying that if I didn't, I could be raped . . . or worse. As he said good-bye to me, Dad pressed his red and white rosary into my hands and told me that my faith in God would protect me. I told my father I loved him, and he promised that he'd pick me up from the pastor's house as soon as it was safe. I lost sight of my mother in the madness around our house and couldn't find her to say good-bye. I never saw my parents alive again.

THERE WERE KILLERS ALL OVER THE COUNTRYSIDE, and Augustine and I barely managed to avoid a group of heavily armed Hutu villagers as we ran to Pastor Murinzi's.

Although he was a Hutu, Pastor Murinzi had been a family friend for many years, and he did agree to hide me. However, as he'd already taken in several other Tutsi women and girls, he couldn't protect Augustine or my brother Vianney, who showed up later. (Damascene had also stopped by, but he'd decided to take shelter with a Hutu friend of his named Bonn.)

"I have no place for them, and hiding men is more dangerous than hiding women," the pastor explained. "I'm taking a horrible risk as it is; if they find any of you here, they will kill us all." My pleas and tears would not change his mind. Thank God my brother Aimable was 3,000 miles away, at school in Senegal, and had escaped the nightmare into which the rest of us had been thrust. The hardest thing I ever had to do was tell Vianney and Augustine that they had to leave the pastor's and try to avoid the killers as best they could on their own. My heart broke as they disappeared into the darkness, not knowing where they would go or if they would find safety.

Pastor Murinzi agreed to hide six Tutsis—myself, a woman and two of her daughters, and two other girls—in a tiny, seldom-used bathroom at the far end of his bedroom. Here, he was able to keep us concealed from the killers, his servants, and even his own family. Two other women joined us later in a room that measured about four feet by three feet, and we were squeezed together so tightly that we could hardly breathe.

Since the pastor had given us strict orders not to talk to one another, fearing that we might be overheard, we barely spoke a word for three months. Yet we had no trouble hearing the crazed monsters outside as they circled the village, chanting while they hunted Tutsis: "Kill them! Kill them! Kill them all! Kill the old and kill the small! Kill every last cockroach!"

For the next 91 days, those seven ladies and I huddled atop each other in that cramped little space while the killers rampaged outside. We could hear reports coming from the radio in the pastor's bedroom that government officials were ordering all the Hutus in Rwanda to pick up a machete and exterminate every Tutsi they saw—even if it was their own husband, wife, or child. Failing to kill Tutsis, or offering them sanctuary, was punishable by death. There were nearly seven million Hutus in the country and, with few exceptions as far as we knew, everyone who was capable of murder had joined in the slaughter.

From international news programs, we learned that the world had turned its back on Rwanda. All but a handful of United Nations (UN) peacekeepers had left, and nobody was coming to our rescue—none of the other African countries, no European nations, and certainly not the United States. Everyone knew what was happening here, but no one acted to stop it. The extremist Hutu government interpreted the silence as a green light to commit genocide, and they proceeded to kill with greater speed and efficiency than even Adolf Hitler had.

We didn't need a radio to know how near death we always were, since the killers searched the pastor's house many times. We heard them cursing on the other side of the thin plaster wall as they pushed over furniture and poked ceiling tiles to see if anyone was in the rafters. The bathroom door was in plain view to anyone in the pastor's bedroom—that our hiding place was never discovered was a miracle of God Himself.

One day as the killers were making their way toward the pastor's, I had a vision of a tall dressing bureau placed in front of the bathroom door. I knew it had to be a sign from God, so I begged Pastor Murinzi to move his bureau in front of the door. He agreed, and no sooner had he done so than the killers burst into his bedroom and searched it from top to bottom again. We could hear them rifling through the bureau, muttering about how they'd found and killed Tutsi babies who had been hidden in drawers. But they didn't look behind the bureau, so our lives were saved.

This was just one of many miracles I experienced during the genocide; the greatest of them all was discovering the true essence of God and, through Him, finding the power to forgive even those who had committed such unspeakable acts against my country and my people.

From the moment I entered that bathroom, I clung to the red and white rosary my father had given me as a parting gift. That rosary became my lifeline to the Lord, and I prayed with it frequently, begging to be spared from rape and murder. But my prayers lacked power because I continued to hate the killers for what they were doing. The more I prayed, the more aware I became that, in order to receive God's true blessing, my heart had to be ready to receive His love. But how could He enter my heart when it was holding so much anger and hatred?

I said the Lord's Prayer hundreds of times, hoping to forgive the killers who were murdering all around me. It was no use—every time I got to the part asking God to "forgive those who trespass against us," my mouth went dry. I couldn't say the words because I didn't truly embrace the feeling behind them. My inability to forgive caused me even greater pain than the anguish I felt in being separated from my family, and it was worse than the physical torment of being constantly hunted.

After weeks of continual prayer, God came to me one night and touched my heart. He made me understand that we are all His children and therefore all deserving of forgiveness. Even those who had done things as wicked and depraved as the killers who were ripping Rwanda apart deserved forgiveness. Like naughty children, they needed to be punished . . . but they also needed to be forgiven.

I then had a vision of Jesus on the cross, using his last breath to forgive his persecutors; for the first time, I was able to completely open myself to let him fill my heart with his power of forgiveness. God's love flooded my soul, and I forgave those who had sinned, and continued to sin, in such unspeakable and unholy ways. The anger and hatred that had hardened my heart vanished, and I was overcome with a deep sense of peace. It no longer mattered to me if I died. I didn't want to, of course, but I knew I was ready. The Lord had cleansed my heart, and I no longer had to fear death, for He had saved my soul. Although I had believed in God and had been praying to Him, Jesus, and the Virgin Mary my entire life, I had never felt His power in me more than at that moment when my heart learned to forgive. Now I felt that power all around me, and I knew that He would be with me for all of my days.

I spent my remaining weeks in the bathroom in prayer and relative peace. The radio reported that the Tutsi rebels of the RPF had followed their leader, Paul Kagame, into Rwanda from their base in Uganda. They'd been fighting the Hutu army since the other women and I had gone into hiding, and now the Hutu government was collapsing. The organizers of the genocide had left Kigali on the run, and the Hutu army was near defeat. The killers were still prowling everywhere, but now there was hope that rescue might be possible.

AFTER THE LADIES AND I HAD SPENT THREE MONTHS IN HIDING, French troops arrived in western Rwanda to set up safe zones, places where Tutsi survivors could find protection and shelter. Although Tutsis largely distrusted the French because they'd long supported the Hutu government with money and weapons, at this point we had no choice but to run to them.

Pastor Murinzi told us that the killers were closing in on our hiding place, and if we didn't leave, we'd certainly be discovered and killed. He smuggled us to a nearby French refugee camp on a moonless night, and the women and I spent several weeks there in relative safety, eating the first real food we'd had since the genocide began. As I encountered other survivors, I slowly learned the extent of the evil that had overtaken my country . . . and I learned about the fate of my family.

My father had been shot to death on the orders of a Hutu official who had once been his good friend. Dad had gone to the local government office to ask the man to help the refugees camped in front of our home, and he was shot in the back as he left the office. He was killed just days after the genocide had begun.

My mother had managed to hide for a little while, but when she thought she heard my brother Damascene calling for help, she ran out into the open to find him. Men who had once been close to our family chopped her to death.

Damascene had indeed been sheltered for many weeks by Bonn, his best friend since childhood. However, while trying to get to a boat on Lake Kivu that would take him to Zaire, my brother was waylaid by killers. He was executed by machete by a gang of local men and boys who were led by a Protestant Hutu minister. People who witnessed Damascene's murder later told me that he'd prayed for the men who were killing him, even as he was being hacked limb from limb.

And finally, there came news of my younger brother, Vianney, whom I'd sent away from the pastor's house with his friend Augustine. After leaving the pastor's, the boys ran to a local soccer stadium and joined thousands of other Tutsis hoping to find safety there. But the stadium became a mass grave when some killers tossed hand grenades onto the field and then sprayed the fleeing crowd with machine-gun fire. A girl who was with Vianney during the attack said that the bullets cut him in half.

What I heard about my family was almost too much for me to bear, but the new and powerful relationship I'd forged with God helped me through my pain. I harbored no anger toward my family's killers; I knew that they'd been possessed by the devil and would have to make their peace with the Lord on Judgment Day.

GOD CONTINUED TO PROTECT ME AFTER THE GENOCIDE, guiding me safely to a new home in Kigali and a new job at the UN. I was able to earn enough money to travel back to Mataba to bury my mother and Damascene, the only family members whose bodies I could find.

I'd made a fresh start, but one thing remained for me to truly make a new life: I needed to practice what God had taught me in hiding by fully forgiving my family's killers. So, in a prison near my hometown, I went to see Felicien, a man whose machete had struck both Mom and Damascene.

Like so many others who had become killers, Felicien's soul was in turmoil. When the evil fog had finally lifted from his heart, all he had left was remorse and guilt. He'd been a tall, proud man whom I'd admired as a child—a business leader and local politician who wore nice suits and always paid attention to his appearance but now his body was decaying and his mind was on the verge of madness. Groveling on the ground before me and unable to look me in the eyes, he was too consumed with shame and regret to ask for my pardon, which I could see he desperately wanted.

Standing in that prison, I knew that Felicien and I, both killer and survivor, were on the same path. We both needed the healing power of God's forgiveness to move forward if our country was to survive and rise from the bitterness, blood, and suffering of the holocaust.

With all of my heart, I forgave Felicien. And I believe that, in his heart, he accepted my forgiveness.

My soul was free and my love of God was overflowing, but my life as a genocide survivor had just begun. Like Rwanda, I would face many dark days and doubts on the path toward an uncertain future, but I knew that this journey would always be blessed if it was traveled with faith.

❖ ❖

CHAPTER 2

WALKING THROUGH THE RUINS

The genocide was over, but the war inside me seemed to keep raging.

As the summer of 1994 drew to a close, my country was still in chaos, my world had been turned upside down, and I thought that I might never breathe easily again. Everything I had known was gone, and everything I saw was changing before my eyes. Approximately two million Hutus had fled into exile across Rwanda's borders, fearing that holocaust survivors would kill them for revenge. And hundreds of thousands of killers and genocide organizers were either dead, captured, or regrouping in the thick jungles of Zaire.

Then there were the victims, for which the count kept going up: at first it was set at 200,000, then 500,000 . . . finally, it would end up at more than a million dead. More than a million innocent Tutsi men, women, and children had been murdered! They had been killed by machete, spear, fire, and gun. They had been brought down by clubs, tortured with knives, and sexually assaulted with broken bottles. The methods were as low-tech as they were efficient and cruel. But no matter how death came to them, my immediate family was all dead and gone, as were countless Tutsi neighbors, relatives, and friends.

Before the genocide, Rwanda was teeming with life: more than a million Tutsis lived side by side with several million Hutus, and villages and towns crowded every hilltop and lined every valley in the land. But now the country was deserted; since only a couple hundred thousand Tutsis had survived, if that, there were more ghosts in Rwanda than people.

Nevertheless, I felt extremely fortunate. I'd survived, no one was hunting me, I'd found a job at the UN, and my friend Sarah's kind parents had welcomed me into their home. Unlike so many thousands of other female Tutsis, I hadn't been tortured or maimed; nor had I been raped and left with an unwanted pregnancy, HIV, or both.

After three months of semistarvation, my weight and my health were returning. And miraculously, some of my family *had* survived: my aunts and cousins in Kibuye were recovering from their ordeal during the genocide, and my brother Aimable was alive and well in Senegal and would be reunited with me before too long.

The Lord had answered my prayers and had led me through great hardship, and my job was giving me pleasure and even moments of joy. Yet as I was quickly learning, the reality of post-holocaust life was a constant series of struggles. Yes, God had blessed me, but my loneliness remained ever sharp, a thorn in my heart.

In the mornings I was picked up by a UN minibus and driven to work, unless I decided to brave the streets and walk. My days in the office were spent surrounded by people who hadn't been born in Rwanda, and I liked to close my eyes and lose myself in the babble of languages of these strangers from distant lands. It was easy to pretend that I was far, far away from my blood-soaked native soil.

But walking home in the evenings, I found it impossible to avert my eyes from what had happened. There was no way to ignore the horrible things that had been done to my people—pretending to be somewhere else wouldn't take me away from the bombed-out or half-burned houses that comprised the new architecture of Kigali. If I dared to look inside the crumbling buildings,

I'd likely find the bodies of an entire family rotting on the floor. As it was, I occasionally had to step over dismembered limbs lying in the road, and I'd see soldiers shooting at dogs that were feeding on human remains.

The dead had become such a health risk to the living that the government declared an official body-removal day—businesses shut down, and everyone was supposed to meet in groups to help carry the corpses to disposal trucks. I'd seen too many bodies by then, so I chose instead to spend the day on my knees, praying for the souls of the deceased.

WHEN I WALKED HOME FROM WORK, I handed coins to men and women on the street whose arms or legs had been hacked off during the massacre. There were so many that I'd usually run out of what little money I had before making it back to Sarah's house.

When I started recognizing the faces looking up at me for help, I realized that the scenes of horror had become familiar. Suffering that was once unimaginable in my country was now common-place. Worse still was understanding that outside of Rwanda, our tragedy had already been forgotten. More than a million people had been savagely murdered, yet the world had barely blinked.

In Kigali, signs of normalcy were emerging in the midst of the misery. A few vegetable markets reopened; when electricity flickered on for an hour or two, people gathered around a radio to hear a soccer match; and former barkeepers were selling banana beer from the trunks of their cars. None of these activities made much sense to me—watching the aftermath of the genocide mixed with the routines of daily life was unnatural and confusing. My parents and brothers had always been there for me when I needed help or guidance, and I felt lost without them. And living without their warmth and affection made this sad place even more bleak and alien.

How I missed the way we used to gather in our living room after dinner to share the stories of our day, kneel down together at evening prayers, or eagerly await a holiday reunion after my brothers and I had gone off to school. Family love had always held me together; now I was detached, in pieces.

17

It's true that I was living with Sarah and her parents and sib-lings now, and they all went out of their way to be kind to me . . . but was I expected to replace my own family with another? Should I have forgotten that the past ever existed and live my life as though nothing had changed? So often when I thought about my parents and brothers, I couldn't help envisioning the suffering of their last moments, images that made my body tremble and left my heart twisting inside my chest. To distance such painful thoughts, I fantasized that the genocide had been a long, terrible nightmare from which my mom and dad would awaken me with soothing words. But this fantasy became harder to hold on to as reality pressed in around me.

In those first weeks and months, it didn't matter where I was—in the middle of dinner with Sarah's family, sitting in church, or typing up a report at the office—my tears would fall without warn-ing. Just a few weeks after starting work at the UN, I learned that people had started referring to me as "the girl who cries a lot." The nickname wounded me, but it *was* true. I cried for what I'd lost, and I cried over what I'd seen.

These thoughts weighed so heavily on my mind that some mornings I could scarcely summon the energy to push myself from bed. *Why not skip work and stay under the blankets?* I'd ask myself. *Why face another day of sorrow? Someone must know the secret of living with such burdens, but I sure don't!* Somehow I always managed to gather my strength and get to the office, but all day I moved like a robot. I did my job as well as I could and never forgot how lucky I was to have work when so many Rwandans had noth-ing. And while I smiled at my co-workers when they greeted me, and I accepted offers to go for tea or have little conversations, my actions and words felt preprogrammed and false. I tried hard to be cheerful, but my heart mirrored the anguish I saw on the street.

ONE AFTERNOON AS I WAS MAKING MY WAY BACK HOME, my legs wouldn't carry me any farther. I leaned against the charred wall of a deserted house and let myself slide to the ground with a thud. Cars rolled by carrying diplomats to and from the airport; faces stared at me from the windows of evening shuttle buses bringing UN workers to their homes; a military troop carrier roared past, the raucous laughter and cursing of soldiers rising above the whining diesel engine; and two women returning from a newly opened market gossiped about their husbands as they walked by with their groceries swaying on top of their heads.

The world keeps turning, no matter how many have been slaughtered, I thought. *How can people continue? Step over the dead? Walk through the blood? Does no one care? What is the point of suffering though this life if nothing we do matters to anyone else?*

The cold stone of the crumbling wall cut into my back as I watched the daylight drain from the sky. I wanted to sink with the sun as it dropped from the world—I longed to follow it into darkness, leave the pain of life behind, and let my body decay among the ruins while my soul drifted away.

Please, God, take me into Your arms now, I silently pleaded. *You have my dear ones with You already, so why do You want me to stay here in this cruel and ugly place? Why must I suffer trying to survive where it's so lonely when my soul yearns to be with You? I'm ready to come to You now. Please take me . . . I am ready to die.*

All I wanted was to slip out of existence. In my mind I saw Sarah's worried family waiting for me at the supper table, wondering why I was so late. I hoped they wouldn't feel too bad or blame themselves when I never returned to their home. Then I thought about my brother Aimable, but I decided he'd already lost so many loved ones that he could handle the death of one more. Besides, I'd be watching over him anyway.

My spirit was ready for heaven, so I sat without moving and waited to go.

An hour passed, and then two. My legs cramped up, my bottom began to ache from the stones beneath me, and my stomach started growling. I was annoyed by my discomfort—that the needs of my body were distracting me from freeing my soul. I tried to ignore the hunger as I had during my three months in hiding, but my stomach only growled more loudly. I guess I'd become used to eating because I suddenly couldn't stop thinking about food.

Again I found myself picturing Sarah and her family at the table, but now I wondered what her mom had prepared for dinner.

Ah, how humiliating to have my resolve overruled by my belly!

But I refused to give in to physical want, so I kept my mind and body still and my eyes tightly closed. My thoughts slowly dissolved into nothingness, and I fell into a dream. Suddenly, an angelic voice was ringing in my ears: "Stand up, Immaculée. You are still alive, and you need to move on! Look for God in all things, and don't despair when your heart aches. God will always be there for you, and you can ask Him for any favor—with Him, all is possible. Now stand up!"

When I opened my eyes, my heart was dancing, and my spirit lifted me up off the ground. I drank in the evening sky that was brushing Kigali with a thousand shades of pink, and I was filled with gratitude.

How beautiful Your world is, Lord! my soul called out. *Forgive me my despair, light my heart with Your love, and guide my feet along Your path. Thank You for sending Your angel to me. You always reach me in my hour of need; You are such a good Father!*

Brushing the dirt from my dress, I hurried out of the ruined building and made my way home. Along the way, I sang "Amazing Grace" at the top of my lungs, even though people looked at me as though I were mad. A smile spread across my face, and then I laughed loudly as I thought about how God had used a little hunger pang to chase away my dark thoughts. My life was His, and I would live it in His service. Sadness and despair would be part of my life and would overtake me from time to time—that was a fact I had to accept. But I also accepted that God was there for me whether I was in a state of depression or a state of great joy. He was my Father, and all I had to do was call for Him and He would be there.

I ran down the hill to Sarah's house. I couldn't wait to eat.

❖ ❖

CHAPTER 3

MOTHER MARY

As much as I suffered while hiding from the killers in Pastor Murinzi's house, the confining tiled walls of that bathroom had offered me the greatest freedom I had ever known. Long after I'd escaped, I actually found myself yearning to be back in the restrictive space where my mind had nowhere to go but to God.

My seven companions and I hadn't been allowed to talk lest we risk alerting the killers, and the room's narrowness had allowed us only the most minimal movements. My leg muscles had been perpetually cramped, my tailbone had burned from endlessly pressing down against the stone floor, and the air had been so stale and thin that even breathing had been an effort. Yet for all that pain and fear, my soul had never soared higher. During those 91 days in hiding, I'd discovered that physical imprisonment could be spiritually liberating and that there was no greater freedom than the one found through prayer.

Praying was nothing new to me, as my earliest memories are of joining my parents and brothers in the daily prayer sessions at home. Church and Sunday school were also places of prayer for me, as were my Catholic high school and Bible study at my university. As a little girl, whenever I wanted anything special, such as an extra-high mark on an exam or for my brother to score the winning goal in a soccer match, I'd get on my knees and pray to God or the Virgin Mary to deliver it upon request, and in a timely manner. Unlike most kids, I found praying to be rewarding, comforting, pleasurable, and even fun. I could openly and freely talk to God like a friend, and I never felt that I had to hold back my feelings or what was going on in my life.

When I was trapped in the pastor's bathroom, where all I saw was terror in the eyes of the other women and all I heard were the howls of blood-drunk killers, praying took on a new meaning. My mind focused completely on God for hours on end. At first, my petitions were driven by my fear—I simply wanted to stay alive. But later, as I spent longer periods in communion with Him, my prayers transported me to a spiritual level I'd never imagined possible. Praying was no longer a request for Divine intervention; it became my gateway to God, and when I passed through, I felt nothing but the warmth and power of His love. In deep prayer there was no fear, there was no pain, and there were no doubts . . . there was only the light of the Lord and the certainty that He loved and cared for me. I felt the Holy Spirit moving within me, and I could hear God's voice assuring me that He was with me and always would be.

When I wasn't praying, the light dimmed, and the hopelessness and horror of my situation returned. But as the genocide passed from days into weeks, I spent more and more time opening my heart in prayer. Entire days and nights would pass where I sat motionless, with one of the pastor's Bibles in my lap and my father's red and white rosary clasped in my hand, and I wouldn't emerge from my meditation . . . even when the killers were rummaging through the house. During those three months, I formed a relationship with the Lord that sustains me to this day. Whenever I'm in trouble, experiencing doubt, or feeling removed from His presence, prayer is what brings me back to that place of inner spiritual peace I discovered in the bathroom.

In the first months after the genocide, I was so busy surviving —finding food and clothing and then starting my new job at the

UN—that I couldn't devote as much time to God as I wanted. Given all of my new duties and responsibilities, I wasn't even sure how much time He expected me to spend in prayer. Besides, there seemed no time or place in which I could properly thank Him for His many gifts and blessings.

Those gifts included my reunion with my dear friend Sarah. Sarah and I had met when we were students at Lycée de Notre Dame d'Afrique, a Catholic high school for girls in the northern province of Gisenyi. My time at Lycée was wonderfully rewarding for study and friendship, but it was also rather harrowing. Gisenyi, a very Hutu area, was dominated by rabidly anti-Tutsi extremists, and it was also close to the Ugandan border. The civil war between the Hutu government and Tutsi rebels who were based in Uganda had just started, and tribal tensions had never been higher. The school only had a few Tutsi girls, and we all felt frightened and vulnerable.

Rwanda is a patrilineal society, which means that while Sarah's mother is Tutsi, Sarah herself is considered to be Hutu because that's what her father is. Nevertheless, she was always a true friend. "Don't ever worry about difficulties between Hutus and Tutsis, Immaculée," she told me one night in our dorm. "We are sisters, and there will never be problems between us . . . only love."

At the time, there were warnings on the radio about Tutsi rebels staging raids in the area. The broadcast described the rebels as demons with horns and fangs and cautioned Hutus that any Tutsi, no matter how peaceful or trusted, should be considered dangerous and an enemy of the state. Amid such vicious Tutsi fearmongering, Sarah's sensitivity and friendship meant a lot, and we forged a bond that would last a lifetime. After we graduated from Lycée, we went off to university together and became roommates. Her little brother, Augustine, became close pals with my brother Vianney, which was why Augustine was visiting my family's house the weekend the genocide began.

I didn't know that Sarah had survived the genocide until God brought her knocking on the door of Aloise's house one day. (Aloise was a friend I'd made in the French refugee camp after I left the pastor's. We traveled together to Kigali, where she put me up and I landed my job at the UN. There will be much more about her later in the book.) When Sarah found me, we fell into each other's arms, and she invited me to live with her family. Her parents, who had married as teenagers, had been together for 55 years. Both her father, Kayonga, and her mother, Filo, were deeply religious and spent hours together praying in their room. It seemed that whenever I passed their bedroom door, I could hear them whispering the soft strains of "Hail Mary, full of grace."

Knowing that God was held in such esteem in Sarah's house was comforting, but I must confess, I was a little envious that I didn't have a room of my own for prayer. Although the home provided me with a safe and loving sanctuary, it was difficult for me to pray there—it was small by Western standards; and crowded with Sarah's brothers, sisters, nephews, and family friends.

I shared a tiny bedroom with Sarah and her older sister, Rose. The girls and their siblings were far more modern than their parents were, and they never talked about God or prayed openly. So at night I'd get under the blankets, hold on to my father's red and white rosary, and pray in silence. What I really wanted to do was yell out, "Praise God! I love You! Do You hear me, Lord?! Take my sorrows and give me Your blessing!" But I never felt at home enough to speak to God aloud or drop to my knees whenever I needed to talk to Him.

One morning I got up well before dawn, crept into the living room, and knelt down before a little statue of the Virgin Mary that belonged to Sarah's mother. "Blessed Mother, you are the only mom I have now, and I need you to help me find a way to speak with God more openly," I whispered, trying not to wake the family. "I know that God hears our prayers wherever we are and however we say them. But, dear Mother, you know how much I need to feel His love around me. There are so many distractions keeping me from Him. Please . . . I know you'll help me find a place where I can pray all day long."

I snuck back into the bedroom, confident that my prayer would soon be answered.

THE VIRGIN MARY HAD ALWAYS BEEN MY FAVORITE SAINT, and since I thought of her as my mother in heaven, I'd usually turn to her when I was frightened, lonely, or upset. Whenever I prayed to her, I always felt better and got a warm feeling in my chest.

My mind now went back to primary school, when one of my teachers had read us a story about how the Blessed Mother had appeared to three schoolchildren in a little village called Fátima in Portugal, speaking to them and entrusting them with important messages from God! My 11-year-old imagination had caught fire, and I started fantasizing about what it would be like to actually meet Mary in person.

How special everyone would think I am if the mother of God spoke to me, I'd thought. *If I make a pretty place for her to appear, I'm sure that she'll visit Rwanda and even come to our home in Mulubu!*

I was so excited by the idea that I lay awake half the night planning how to prepare for Mary's arrival. By morning I had everything figured out, so I headed off to my friend Jeanette's house to recruit her in my plan.

"The children that Mary visited in Fátima were shepherds, Jeanette, so we're going to have to pretend to be shepherds as well," I said excitedly, explaining my scheme. "After class we'll climb the hill where my father keeps our goats. We'll make a big circle of flowers—the prettiest ones we can find—at the very top of the hill. When Mary looks down and sees us praying in such a beautiful spot, she'll come right down to talk to us!"

My friend was as thrilled as I was but pointed out a serious flaw in the plan: "There were three children at Fátima, Immaculée. Maybe Mary won't come if there are only the two of us."

Jeanette made a good point. To remedy the problem, we convinced her little brother, Fabrice, to come along, even though he was too young to appreciate the significance of the historic role we'd assigned to him.

Every evening for the next week, the three of us followed Mafene, the man who tended my father's goats and cows, as he led the animals to the pasture. At the top of the hill we'd hide behind some bushes so that Mafene wouldn't see us as we picked flowers and laid them out in a circle. Unfortunately, the blooms wilted quickly. We promised each other that we'd come back with a shovel and plant a variety of Rwanda's most beautiful flowers in a huge circle where we could pray with our rosaries until Mary appeared. We told ourselves that thousands of people would come up the hill and stand outside the circle to witness our apparitions—just as they had with the children of Fátima.

Although my friends and I prayed behind the bushes every day, we never got around to planting the circle of flowers, despite how critical it might have been in assuring that the Blessed Mother would come to Mataba. It wasn't long before climbing the hill every day got tiresome. Mary, we assumed, was too busy to come to our village, so we stopped going to the pasture to pray for her to appear.

Three weeks later, my father burst into the house with big news. "There's been a miracle!" he shouted. "The Virgin Mary has appeared to three girls right here in Rwanda! She appeared to them down the road from us in Kibeho."

I was amazed . . . but also heartbroken and angry. *Why hadn't I kept praying?* I chided myself. *We should have planted the circle of flowers three weeks ago!* Later, Jeanette and I cried about our missed opportunity. If we'd only planted the flowers, Mary would have definitely come to Mataba, not Kibeho! She'd obviously visited those children by mistake.

It's a funny story to me now, but it always comes to mind whenever I'm not dedicating enough time to my prayers or following through on work I've set out to do. It was an early lesson in the importance of not losing faith, because, sooner or later, all prayers are answered. It also taught me that we can't expect God to do everything for us just because He hears our prayers—we have to do our part and follow our petitions with action.

Kibeho was a controversial subject in Rwanda because, as with any "miraculous" event, the authenticity of the apparitions that started appearing there in 1981 was questioned. But after 20 years of theological, psychological, and scientific investigation, Bishop Augustine Misago proclaimed that the Kibeho visions of the Virgin

Mary were credible. I myself never had any doubt they were real; nor did the thousands of Rwandans who, like me, made pilgrimages to the village between 1981 and 1989 to hear Mary speak through the three young women whom she'd chosen to deliver her messages.

When the Virgin spoke at Kibeho, she said that she wanted to be known as the "Mother of the Word" and begged people to love each other and return to prayer. Many Rwandans, she warned, were concealing evil in their hearts toward their neighbors, and if they didn't accept God's love, "there will be rivers of blood in Rwanda, and even those who escape it will be sad forever." Yet darkness wouldn't come if people in every town and village picked up their rosaries and prayed for their country with all of their hearts. At times, Mary even sent personal messages to the leaders of the nation through the girls to whom she appeared—but the leaders either didn't hear or didn't heed her words.

If only Rwanda had listened to the messages of Our Lady of Kibeho, the genocide could have been averted.

Soon after I asked the Virgin Mary to help me find a place to spend quiet time with God, Sarah's mom invited me to attend Mass at a chapel I'd never been to before. When we got there, I knew that God had answered my prayers. The chapel was part of the Christus Center, a beautiful Jesuit retreat on the edge of Kigali, nestled in a narrow valley between two hills with a beautiful vista of farms and fallow fields. The grounds of the Christus Center itself overflowed with life: monkeys chattered in nearby banana groves, cows grazed in the distant fields, and flowers bloomed everywhere. I could taste the air on my tongue, sweet with the aroma of blossoming chrysanthemums.

In front of the chapel, I was greeted by a beautiful, life-sized statue of the Blessed Virgin. "You have answered my prayer, haven't you, dear Mother?" I whispered with a smile. "I know that I've been brought here to have time with God and your beautiful son, Jesus. Thank you, Mother, thank you."

The Mass was joyous, and it was the first time I'd heard happy singing in church since the genocide. As the choir raised its collective voice in unison, my scalp tingled with the music. One hymn, "One Day I Will See Your Face, Lord," was much loved by my brother Damascene, who had been an altar boy in his teens. I closed my eyes and let my heart drink in the words and music:

A day will come when I will see Your face, Lord
But now I follow behind You
I will never stumble
I will never fall
For You are there to guide me
I will follow You, Lord

One of the proudest moments of my life had been watching Damascene carry the cross of Jesus as he led the bishop's procession through the center isle of Gisenyi Cathedral, while a 600-member boys' choir sang "One Day I Will See Your Face, Lord." Damascene had gazed up at the cross with such a loving expression that I knew he had God very near to his heart. God was always close to Damascene, and I'm certain He welcomed my brother directly into heaven after the killers chopped him to death with their machetes.

After Mass, I wandered through the Christus Center's garden, marveling at the many different types of flowers. At one point, as I stepped off the path to get a closer look, a nun cried out to me to stop moving and to carefully retrace my steps. "You must walk carefully here, child," she warned. "Yesterday a youngster stepped on a grenade that had been tossed into the garden during the war, and the poor boy was killed. Even the most beautiful places in Rwanda have no end of tragedy.

"Much blood was spilled here minutes after the killing began," she continued, leading me to a room where the killings had taken place. The walls and ceiling were still caked with dried blood, and a large wooden cross leaned precariously against the wall.

"We lost 17 of our brothers and sisters in the first hour of the genocide," she remarked. "They are with God now."

I said a prayer for the men and women who had been murdered in that wretched room, and a prayer for the boy who'd been
killed the day before—yet another victim of the hatred and violence still haunting Rwanda. *Hold them tightly, Lord.*

As we walked out, I wondered aloud if there was a place near
the garden where I could be by myself for a few moments. "Sister, it's so hard to find a quiet space in Kigali to talk with God," I
explained, as we walked back to the garden, "but it's so peaceful
here. Is there somewhere I can sit alone for a while and pray?"

"Oh yes, my dear, we have exactly what you need."

The nun led me to a long building of narrow rooms at the
edge of the garden and said, "The Christus Center was once quite
famous in Rwanda for the very thing you seek. People, usually
priests, came here from all over the country when they wanted
to reconnect with God . . . no one has come since the killings,
though. We used to take a little rent money for the rooms, but if
you don't have any, the Lord will provide." She gave me a sweet
smile as she opened the door to the room closest to the garden.

The walls were old and cracked but very clean, and there was
a window opening toward the valley with a spectacular pastoral
view. Furnishings were sparse—a single bed, a chair, and a little
writing table—and the space wasn't much larger than the pastor's
bathroom. But without seven other women piled on top of me, it
felt positively palatial.

It was a room of my own, and it would become my spiritual
refuge for months to come. It had two modest adornments: a rect-
angular prayer mat at the side of the bed, and a cream-colored
quilted wall-hanging. Its simple message, which was stitched into
its center with bright red thread, seemed to be placed there especially for me. It read: "Behind every story of true love, there is a
story of great patience."

I sighed happily, knowing that I was exactly where my heart
and soul needed to be.

❖ ❖

CHAPTER 4

PEACE AND PRAYER

No one entered my room at the Christus Center except God and me. It was my private communion chamber, and I disappeared into it every chance I could. Sometimes I was so eager to get there I'd pack an overnight bag at Sarah's on Thursday evening; that way, I could go directly to the center from work on Friday and stay until Sunday night. Whenever I arrived at Christus, my first prayer was always one of gratitude: *Thank You for breathing new life into my heart, Lord. Keep it clean, free from hatred, and always willing to forgive.*

At first the freedom of having my own room was daunting, even overwhelming. My tears must have known that nobody was watching because they sprang from my eyes the moment I shut the door. Thus, the first few weekends at Christus were soggy ones. Being completely alone with God triggered a deep emotional release as painful memories that had been suppressed for too long moved to the center of my consciousness. Sometimes I wept hysterically over what I'd lost; even so, I knew that all those tears had to fall. I also knew with absolute certainty that God does not want us to carry such sorrow through our days.

After long, liberating cries, I'd sit at my window and gaze at the rolling fields in front of me, wondering what it meant to be truly happy. My life had been happy before the genocide, as had the lives of my family and friends. But was it really happiness if it could so easily be snatched away by others? Some men and women I worked with at the United Nations seemed to greatly enjoy romance or shopping, but could genuine happiness depend upon finding physical pleasure, satisfying someone else's desire, or spending money meaninglessly? Even those who'd found happiness celebrating God in church before the genocide now too often sat morosely in their pews, mouthing the most joyous hymns with somber monotony.

The more I thought about happiness, the more I despaired that it had left Rwanda for good, since there was no lightness to be found anywhere. *How will we ever heal without smiles or laughter?* I asked myself. *Then again, how _can_ we laugh after such carnage, when bodies still lie in the street and children continue to be blown apart by discarded grenades?*

Yet God expected us to be happy, and to find our happiness by filling our hearts with His love. Jesus told us this in John 15:9–11: "As the Father has loved me, so have I loved you. Now remain in my love. If you obey my commands, you will remain in my love, just as I have obeyed my Father's commands and remain in his love. I have told you this so that my joy may be in you and that your joy may be complete."

But people had forgotten how to find God's love—they couldn't raise their hearts to Him when their sorrow was pushing them down. *Will Rwandans ever know Your love and joy again, Lord?* I prayed. *How can I be of service to You in this?*

I rested my head on my table, using my Bible to cushion my thoughts and ease my mind. All the answers I was looking for were there in the word of God. I looked up and saw the sun streaming through my little window and noticed that it was warming my skin. As the flowers outside bent toward the light to drink its energy, I realized, *You are the sun, aren't You, God? You are our light, our sustenance.*

I could feel His presence everywhere, from the subtle scent of new life forming in the garden's damp soil to the soft breeze drifting across the valley and gently caressing my face. The infinite magnitude of Creation placed my sadness in context. *God's power is so vast and my strength so puny,* I thought. *Why do I struggle alone with my anguish when I have such a strong God standing by my side, ready to help at the drop of a prayer?* The answer was right there in the Bible, and I already knew it well . . . I didn't have to struggle alone.

Stretching out on the bed, I relaxed my muscles and began a spiritual exercise I'd learned in my university prayer group called "abandonment." Breathing slowly and deeply, I closed my eyes, opened my heart to the Holy Spirit, and allowed my thoughts to drift heavenward. I prayed slowly, pausing between each sentence to hear God's voice in the silence. "Dear Lord, come into my life and take my pain," I said aloud. "I abandon it all to You: every sorrow and sadness, every hurt, every doubt, and every tear. I hand You my heartache; fill me with Your love. Father, Father, Father, Father . . ."

I repeated "Father" many times until I fell asleep. When I awoke I felt so light-headed that I thought I was floating toward the ceiling—I worried that if I didn't hold on to the bed, I would float right out the window and over the valley. God had emptied my soul of sadness; my eyes were dry, and I had a smile on my face. I was happy.

Christus became a spiritual refuge I never wanted to leave. I spent every weekend—and sometimes an evening or two during the week—blissfully shut away in my little room. Much of the time I sat by the window praying with my father's rosary or sitting in the garden reading my Bible.

At times it seemed that my ability to shut out the world and focus on God was nearly absolute. A knock never landed upon my door, no visitor sought me out, and workers didn't disturb me when I meditated in the garden. Guests of the Christus Center were there to commune with the Lord, and everyone was polite enough not to interrupt those conversations. Even my meals in the cafeteria were taken in peaceful reflection; the kitchen staff brought food and cleared dishes wordlessly.

My silence was broken one quiet Saturday afternoon, however. I was reading my Bible in the garden when I noticed an older priest standing in front of the statue of the Virgin Mary. Without thinking, I yelled so loudly my throat hurt: *"Father Bugingo! Father Bugingo!"*

Jumping to my feet, I ran to the statue as quickly as I could, crossing the lawn in a few giant strides. "Father Bugingo!" I called. "Is it really you?"

"Immaculée! It's so good to see you, child," the priest said warmly, offering me his right hand to shake in greeting.

I wanted to jump into his arms and hug him with all my strength, but I knew better. Instead, I shook his hand and replied, "I thank God you're alive, Father."

Father Jean Baptiste Bugingo was one of the most beloved priests ever to lecture at my high school. He was a professor at the seminary at Damascene's college, which wasn't far from the all-girls Catholic school I'd attended, and sometimes priests from the seminary were invited to our chapel to conduct evening Mass. While it was always a treat to have a guest preacher, news of Father Bugingo's arrival would cause quite a ruckus on campus. Girls would crowd into the bathroom before Mass and jostle each other for space in the mirror to apply a touch of contraband lipstick or rouge—both officially frowned upon by the Mother Superior. In fact, the first time I heard Father Bugingo's name was while two of my dormmates bickered over which one of them he liked best.

"The last time he was here, he looked at me three times during Mass. I'm sure he knows how pious I am," a girl named Josephine claimed.

"Oh, please," her friend Marianne protested with a laugh. "I've met Father Bugingo personally and told him exactly how often I pray. I'm going to make sure I'm in the front pew when he arrives so that he knows I'm there!"

It was quite a buildup, but when Mass finally commenced, I was confused about all the fuss. *What's the big deal about Father*

Bugingo? I wondered, shaking my head as an exceptionally thin but otherwise nondescript man walked into the chapel. *Why are they all acting like he's some kind of movie star or something?*

But as soon as he spoke, I was an instant member of his fan club. I had never heard anyone talk about love with such eloquence, conviction, and passion before; and I was mesmerized by his words.

"Our desire to love is stamped on our hearts before we are born. You must not let life erase it! God knew you in the womb, and He planted your ability to love in your soul before you drew your first breath. You must nurture that seed, allowing it to grow strong within you. You must love your family and love your neighbors; above all, you must love God. God doesn't just want you to love; He commands it. He commands it!" Father Bugingo boomed, his penetrating voice rolling over the parish of wide-eyed schoolgirls in a hypnotic wave.

The priest's sermon was all about how faith and love can overcome evil and despair, using Jewish holocaust survivor Martin Gray as an example of how a heart steeped in faith can withstand anything. Although I was an honor student, I'd never heard of the Jewish holocaust until that point. Later, I attributed the gap in my education to the extremist Hutu politicians who'd shaped our curriculum—they'd kept us ignorant about genocide until they'd made us victims of one.

Father Bugingo told us about Martin Gray's commitment to live a life driven by love, even after he witnessed the horrible deaths of his mother and two brothers in a Nazi concentration camp. Years later, Gray lost his wife and four children in a forest fire . . . and he still didn't give up.

"Martin Gray has lived his life with love," Father Bugingo preached. "He wasn't beaten down by the horror of genocide, and he wasn't motivated by hatred or revenge after he escaped. He let his heart live and started a family of his own. When a fire killed his loved ones, he didn't despair—he dedicated himself to forest conservation. Life did not erase the love God stamped on his heart, no matter how much suffering it sent his way. Follow his example; live your life as Martin Gray did."

After that sermon, all the girls flocked around this special priest outside the church. Many of them hoped to give him a hug and a kiss on the cheek, but he kept them all at arm's length. "Don't forget that I'm a priest, ladies," he said with a laugh. "A handshake is as much scandal as I permit. Give your affection to God and each other."

Over the years I kept in touch with Father Bugingo through my brother Damascene, who teasingly suggested that I had a crush on the kindly priest. Damascene was partly correct—I loved Father Bugingo's fierce belief in love and his passion for God. His sermon had moved me so much that I went on to consult with him on all questions of faith. To this day, he remains my most trusted spiritual advisor.

When I stumbled upon him at the Christus Center, I was ecstatic to find that someone else I knew had survived, especially someone I loved so much.

We sat chatting in the garden for the rest of the afternoon, and I confided all to him: the fear of being hunted; the loss of my family; my anger and doubts; my depression and thoughts of suicide; and, of course, the way God continued to heal me.

Father Bugingo told me how the Interahamwe had forced its way into his church and murdered every Tutsi parishioner. He was able to survive through the kindness of an elderly Belgian nun who risked her life to hide him in her ceiling. There was a price on the priest's head because he was such a respected Tutsi, and the Interahamwe hunted him night and day. But with God's help, he managed to walk several miles to safety without being seen by the killers. He, too, would learn that his family—his parents, sister, and nieces—had all died in the slaughter.

Since Father Bugingo's grief was as great as mine, I didn't dare ask him for the counsel I so desperately wanted. But he was such an intuitive priest and natural therapist that he just looked into my eyes and knew. "How can I help you, dear?" he asked quietly, placing his hand on top of mine.

"Oh, Father, I feel so at peace sitting in this garden with you, but it's very difficult for me to live in this country now. Rwanda has become so ugly . . . I only want to stay in the garden or sit in my room and pray. I never want to leave."

"We'd all like that," he replied, "but we can't hide from what happened. Keep in mind that you're not nearly as wounded as most survivors are, and God needs your strength to help others. There have been times when even I have wanted to leave all this sorrow behind. Being a priest is not easy in Rwanda now; people see my collar and scream, 'Where was God when my family was being killed?! Where was Jesus when my child was being raped?! Why did God abandon Rwanda?!'"

"I've heard people say that, too, Father."

"God *didn't* abandon our country, Immaculée. He was here the entire time, feeling the pain of every victim. He is still here—He is with the wounded, the lost, and the grieving. Yes, it's ugly in Rwanda, but God's beauty is still alive here. And you will find it in love."

"But my entire family is gone! Whom can I love now?"

"Go back into the world and find someone to bless with that same type of love," he told me. "Give it to someone who has no love at all, such as the homeless, the sick, or the orphaned. Look for the beauty of God in the eyes of a little boy or girl. Find a child whose heart has been shattered, and give him or her some happiness. Remember, all love begins with a smile."

CHAPTER 5

THE POWER OF UNCONDITIONAL LOVE

Father Bugingo's words moved me deeply. There was great truth in what he'd said about finding love by giving it to the weak, lonely, and poor. My brother Damascene, for instance, was able to do so in places and hearts that most others avoided.

Damascene's humor, witty intelligence, and easy manner had made him one of the most popular youths in our region. He enjoyed life so much that everybody wanted to be with him to share in his happiness. Whenever he returned home from college during the holidays, people came from all over to see him. He received countless invitations to visit other people's homes and had a constant stream of visitors at ours. If my other brothers and I hadn't loved him so much, I'm sure we would have been really jealous.

"What are you doing to make so many people like you, Damascene? Are you giving away all our money?" our mother would tease. She was proud of her son's charisma and knew it was his heart that drew people to him.

"They visit me to get a look at you," Damascene would reply, winking at Mom. He was never bigheaded or boastful about his popularity, and he offered his friendship freely—he was as comfortable talking with professors and priests as he was speaking with the homeless or sick. And he'd often disappear for hours, making social calls to people who otherwise didn't have a friend.

Damascene never mentioned these little visits to anyone, and I only found out about them when I saw Nyinawindinda, a village vagrant who lived in a lean-to and was so filthy that flies buzzed around her. After I spotted her wearing one of my brother's best shirts one day, I asked her where she'd found it, worried that Damascene had been hurt on his way home or had lost his travel bag.

"Your brother is a good boy, Immaculée," she answered. "He always brings me such beautiful presents."

When I asked Damascene about the shirt, he said that he'd given it to Nyinawindinda because he didn't have any money in his pocket when he visited her. Little did he know that Nyinawindinda's parents had left her one of the largest tracts of land in the area. My family never tired of teasing Damascene after Nyinawindinda showed up at our house one day wanting to sign the property over to him for his kindness.

"Damascene is my only friend, and I want to give him a present," Nyinawindinda told my father, after he explained that Damascene couldn't accept such an expensive gift. Later I discovered that my brother had many such friends, but he never talked about them. He loved unconditionally, and was unconditionally loved in return.

The night I saw Father Bugingo, Damascene came to me in a dream, as he had many times after the genocide when my heart was aching. He'd often smile and tell me to stop crying because he could hear my sobs in heaven. Sometimes I'd wake myself up laughing because he seemed so annoyed to be taken away from paradise to comfort his little sister. But at the end of each dream, he'd always say something like, "Immaculée, stop being so sad. Don't you know that Mom, Dad, Vianney, and I didn't die? We are alive and will see you soon."

But on this particular night, my brother didn't say anything—he just appeared to me with two young boys, who stood on either side of him holding his hands. The boys reminded me of two orphaned brothers I'd cared for while staying at the French refugee camp. I really loved those little boys but had lost track of them after they were shipped to another camp. In the dream, they were happy and safe with Damascene.

The next morning after Sunday Mass, I ran into a young man standing in front of Mother Mary's statue. He looked familiar, so I smiled at him as I walked by.

"Immaculée, what's the matter with you? Don't you recognize me?"

For the second day in a row, I disrupted the peace and quiet at Christus with a cry of happiness. "Oh, Ganza! You made it, too! It's so wonderful to see you!" I exclaimed, now recognizing a family member I hadn't seen for years.

Ganza Jean Baptiste was a cousin on my mother's side who'd grown up in Goma, a town in Zaire that borders Rwanda on the north shore of Lake Kivu. Ganza's parents had fled to Goma during the Hutu Revolution of 1959, and they lived too far away for us to visit. However, when Ganza's family moved back to Rwanda when he was a teenager, my cousin and I became friends. Now he was clearly as delighted as I was to find a living relative, but his eyes told me that he was carrying a personal tragedy just like the rest of us were.

The questions flooded out of me: "What are you doing here? Where are your sisters? How did you survive?"

It turned out that Ganza had been teaching French at a Jesuit college in Zaire when the genocide started. Returning to Rwanda afterward, he found that his mother and too many relatives and friends to count had been murdered. I took my cousin's hand in mine; we shared the same pain. We talked about what had happened to our country, our lives, and our loved ones. His father had died years before, so, like me, Ganza had been orphaned by the holocaust. Miraculously, we'd both come to the Christus Center to connect with God.

"After what happened, all I felt was hatred," Ganza explained. "My life was over, and I couldn't see a future. But one day I just knew that God was the only way . . . and that's why I'm here. I've come to study with the Jesuits because God has called me. I'm going to become a priest, Immaculée."

I gave him a hug and said, "Your mother would be so proud."

Rwanda was in dire need of new priests and pastors. The genocide had turned the clergy into killers and victims, and churches—which had always provided sanctuary to Tutsis during earlier acts of genocide—had been among the worst killing fields in the country. Entire communities had been betrayed by their church leaders and slaughtered in the pews by the thousands.

Little wonder, then, that the Masses I attended after the genocide lacked feeling. So many Rwandans had lost faith—the houses of God had burned with the rest of the country. The country now needed men and women who truly loved the Lord to rebuild its churches and its faith. Rwanda needed people like my cousin.

"You'll be a good soldier for God, Ganza. You'll help bring back the light."

"Not everyone wants me to do this," he replied. "My brothers and sisters who survived want me to forget about God and look for a wife. They want me to make babies and help build the family back up."

"When you become a priest, you'll have many children."

"I have many children now, Immaculée. I spend a lot of time with the orphans at Mother Teresa's. You should go visit there sometime, since the children need all the love they can get."

Suddenly I felt God's presence all around me. Father Bugingo had told me to give my love to an orphaned child, Damascene had shown me my lost orphan boys, and now Ganza was directing me to an orphanage.

I looked up at the statue of the Virgin Mary. *God does work in mysterious ways,* I thought, *but sometimes He makes things pretty obvious.*

I WALKED UP AND DOWN THE HILLS OF KIGALI THAT AFTERNOON, making my way from the Christus Center to the Home of Hope, the orphanage my cousin had told me about that was run by the Missionaries of

Charity, the Sisters of Mother Teresa of Calcutta. Everyone I stopped to ask for directions simply referred to it as "Mother Teresa's."

"Mother Teresa," I murmured. It was a name I loved to say aloud.

When I was in high school, my dormmates often teased me in a friendly way for praying so much. Even though I loved singing and dancing with them, I developed a reputation for being overly pious and in constant communion with God. When word got around school about my hobby, I was asked to stay after class to meet with one of the nuns. I couldn't imagine why, but I thought I was in trouble.

"I understand you spend a lot of your free time praying, Immaculée," Sister Michelle stated.

"Yes, that's true, but I don't see why there should be anything wrong with that."

"Don't be silly! Of course there's nothing wrong with praying," she said, smiling broadly as she placed a cassette tape on the desk in front of me. "I don't know if you're meant to be a nun, but I definitely think you have a calling. God has something in mind for you, so don't ever be embarrassed to talk to Him through prayer. You never know when He might tell you what He is expecting from you. And I can guarantee that someday God will be the only friend you'll have to talk to. Anyway, go ahead and listen to this tape; if you like it, I'll get you another one."

The cassette was about the life of Saint Francis of Assisi, and I was hooked immediately. It turned out that Sister Michelle had a large selection of saints' stories on tape—within two weeks, I'd listened to the biographies of Saint Joan of Arc, Saint Augustine of Hippo, and Saint Thérèse of Lisieux. Then I pestered her for more.

After I'd exhausted Sister Michelle's collection (and her patience), she gave me a book about Mother Teresa, telling me, "I've written to friends in Belgium for new tapes, but try reading about Mother Teresa in the meantime. I think you'll find her as inspiring as any saint."

Sister Michelle was right. After reading about Mother Teresa's devotion to God and her work with the poor, I thought of her as a living saint. She actually came to Africa that year and established chapters of her order, the Missionaries of Charity, in several countries.

Mother Teresa even came to Rwanda! During her visit to Kigali, church officials took her to the top of the city's highest hill so that she could see the steeples of the finest churches. She pointed to a valley, where a patchwork of cardboard roofs stretched over dozens of city blocks, and asked, "What is that?"

"We're working to get rid of that, Mother," one of the officials answered. "We're trying to improve the lives of the people, but that is our biggest slum."

"Then that's where I'll sleep tonight," she said, and requested to be taken there immediately.

Apparently the officials thought that sleeping in a Kigali slum would have been more dangerous than sleeping in a Calcutta slum, so they wouldn't give in to Mother Teresa's request. But the story stayed with me, as did the words she used to describe the mission she envisioned for her order when she founded it in Calcutta in 1950. She told her followers that if they stayed with her, they must love and care for "the hungry, the naked, the homeless, the crippled, the blind, the lepers, all those people who feel unwanted, unloved, uncared for throughout society, people that have become a burden to the society and are shunned by everyone."

I rested for a moment at the crest of the last hill I had to climb before reaching the orphanage. Looking down at Kigali, I could see the same slum Mother Teresa had looked upon years before. But now the entire city was a slum—*everyone* lived in pain, poverty, and illness.

I half walked, half slid down the steep hill leading to the orphanage's big blue gate, and then I knocked on the metal bars.

"Are you all right, child? Are you in trouble? Do you need help?" asked the kindly nun who opened the gate. She was wearing the blue and white habit Mother Teresa wore, the same one worn by all the nuns who belonged to the Missionaries of Charity.

"No, Sister, I'm fine," I replied. "My cousin Ganza told me about the orphanage, and I want to come be with the children. Will you let me meet them?"

The nun invited me inside, calling for another nun to let the children know they had a visitor. As we chatted in the yard, I could see that the situation at the orphanage was desperate. The grounds were littered with debris and broken glass, and there were signs of artillery bombardment from the war. Clouds hung over the city, and the sullen afternoon light infused the orphanage with a sadness I could feel in my bones, a feeling belied by the nun's warm and welcoming face.

She followed my gaze as I looked around the desolate yard, commenting, "We do what we can here. Children and infants are dropped at our door every day . . . there are so many. We do for them what we can with what God provides, but all we have to give them right now is a little food and a lot of love. Love is what they need most, so I hope you have plenty to give."

At the far end of the yard stood yet another statue of the beautiful Virgin Mary, this time draped in the blue and white clothing of Mother Teresa. I looked at the wee Baby Jesus Mary was cradling in her arms, smiled, and silently prayed, *Thank you for guiding me here, Mother. I know that you're always watching out for me. Please help me be of service to these children.* Aloud, I said, "Yes, Sister, I brought all of my love with me."

The other nun returned and guided me through several long cinder-block rooms that were lined with narrow metal beds. As my eyes adjusted to the light, I realized that there were dozens of young faces staring up at me from the beds.

"There are so many children and so few beds. These are some of our sickest residents," the nun explained. We stopped by the bedside of a young boy whose right arm had been hacked off by a machete, and his stump was wrapped in bloodied gauze.

"Hello, sweetheart," I said, sitting beside him and taking his left hand in mine.

The boy looked into my face. There were no tears; he met my eyes and stared back blankly.

"It's okay," I assured him. "You don't have to say anything. We'll have lots of time to talk later. I'm going to be here all the time to see you."

The boy gave me a tentative smile, rested his head against my arm, and gently squeezed my hand.

"If you do what you promise—if you visit frequently—you'll be a welcome friend," the nun told me. "You can come with food and clothing, but make sure that you always come with love. If you can put a smile on a child's face, you'll have our blessing."

She then led me through other rooms crowded with ailing and wounded youngsters. I cradled infants whose lungs were filled with fluid, whose skin was completely blistered, and whose eyes were left sightless by the virus passed to their mothers by Interahamwe rapists.

"We find an AIDS baby at the gate several times a week," the nun said. I knew that in the years to come, Rwanda would be inundated with children of genocide born carrying a disease used as a weapon of ethnic extermination.

"We never turn anyone away, no matter how old, young, or sick they might be," she continued, taking me to a larger room to meet another group of children. "I don't want you to be overwhelmed by sadness on your first visit, my dear. Know that wherever there are children, you can at least find some happiness. Happiness is like a weed—with a little light, it will grow anywhere."

As I stepped through the doorway into the main common room, a great cheer rose up to the ceiling and lifted my spirits to the rafters.

About 200 children, most under the age of seven, stood in a semicircle waiting to greet me. A nun lifted her hand, and the children began to sing:

> *Welcome good guest, welcome kind guest,*
> *You are a welcome, kind guest to our home.*
> *Welcome kind guest, welcome good guest,*
> *You are welcome to call this house home.*

The children ended the song with another cheer, and the semi-circle closed around me. For the next few hours I ran around and played like a kid myself—singing, skipping rope, and reading stories with as many boys and girls as possible. By the time the supper bell rang, I was physically exhausted but spiritually energized.

I closed my eyes, listened to the laughter around me, and thought, *Thank you, Mother Mary, for bringing me here . . . and thank you, Jesus, for these little children.*

As she escorted me out of the orphanage, the nun rested her hand on my shoulder and looked into my eyes. "Now, don't forget you made a promise to come back soon. You've given these children something today; don't take it away with you."

"Sister, these children have given me more than I will ever be able to give them in return," I replied. "This is my new home. I'll be back tomorrow after work, and I'll be here every chance I get."

I started to say good-bye and then realized that I hadn't learned the name of a single boy or girl.

"Sister, wait!" I shouted as the gate closed. "I don't know any of their names!"

"Names don't matter here, child. They're all children of God."

CHAPTER 6

A NEW TYPE OF HEARTACHE

Like so many other Rwandans, the pain and horror of the genocide had driven one of my oldest friends mad.

When we were little girls growing up in Mataba, Jeanette had been my dearest companion and most trusted confidante, who affectionately called me "Imma." Because I had three brothers, I yearned for the special bond I'd seen between sisters. Jeanette and I liked each other so much that we had no problem pretending to be sisters; eventually, we became so close that we forgot we were pretending.

As I mentioned earlier, Jeanette had happily joined my plan to become a visionary by trying to entice the Virgin Mary to appear to us. Another time we decided to run away and join a convent, but the priest in charge told us to come back when we were 18. We always tried very hard to be good girls—not to gain favor with our teachers or parents, but to make God and Mother Mary proud of us.

Jeanette wasn't the best scholar in the village, but she tried harder than anyone to get good grades. When we weren't off on adventures together, I'd make her sit down and study with me. Whenever other kids teased my friend about her marks, I'd jump to her defense, my face hot with anger. No one could pick on Jeanette or make her feel bad when I was around. One of the reasons why I studied so hard was so I could get a good job when I grew up and take care of her.

"Sisters should live together," we'd say, promising that we'd always stick together.

Although I made other good friends as time went by, Jeanette and I remained close right up until I went away to high school. And even then, we stayed in touch through letters and spent lots of time together during holidays.

Jeanette was at university in Zaire when the genocide erupted, which saved her life. But her parents and six siblings—not to mention numerous aunts, uncles, cousins, nieces, and nephews—had all been murdered. She was the sole survivor of her family, the last of her bloodline.

When I discovered that my dear friend was in Kigali, I went to see her immediately. I was so thrilled that we'd be able to make our childhood dream of being sisters and living together come true at last.

She was staying at a boardinghouse, and as soon as I stepped through the door, I hugged her as tightly as I could. But for some reason, she didn't really hug me back—in fact, she felt like dead weight in my arms. Tears of joy were rolling down my cheeks, but Jeanette's eyes were dry.

Oh well, she's just tired, I told myself, as we sat down on the edge of her bed.

I started talking nonstop about all the terrible events that had come to pass since we'd last seen each other: what had happened to our families and all of our friends, the problems back home in Mataba, what was going on in Rwanda—everything. Then I told her about the good things that had happened, including how I'd discovered God and the power of His forgiveness, the French refugee camp, and my job at the United Nations.

I talked and talked and talked . . . but Jeanette didn't say a word. She sat staring into space, twisting a lock of her hair, nodding whenever I paused to take a breath. After a while, I was afraid to stop talking; I sensed that if a silence were allowed to come between us, something bad would fill the space. In all the years we'd known each other, I'd never once felt uneasy in Jeanette's presence. But now I was nervous, scared to find out what was wrong with her.

Finally, I ran out of things to say. I put my hands on her shoulders and gently turned her toward me until our eyes met. There was nothing there. This wasn't the girl I knew and loved, the girl who should be unburdening herself of sorrow and pain by sharing it with the person who was once like a sister to her.

"Jeanette, what's the matter? What's going on with you?"

"Oh, nothing," she said absently.

I thought she must be so distraught with grief that she didn't know how to begin talking about the genocide. I took her hands in mine to let her know that she could confide in me as she always had. "Come on, Jeanette, you can tell me anything," I reminded her. "Do you want to talk about what happened to you? What happened to our families? It's so very, very sad."

"Yes, Imma, I know what happened. Yeah, it was pretty sad. But I really love what you've done with your hair. You're doing your braids differently, aren't you?"

What? What in God's name are you talking about? My hair? I thought, completely confused by what my old friend was saying. My heart was aching, and I began to cry. After a few minutes, I convinced myself that it was all in my head—Jeanette was fine, and I was the one who was acting strangely. Maybe I was making her uncomfortable.

I pressed my fists into my eyes, pushed away my tears, and then tried to start the conversation over again with some small talk: "Yes, I did my braids like this for my new job. Do you like it?"

"I do, Imma. Your hair is so beautiful." Then a few minutes later, she asked, "How do you feel about your mom being gone?"

"Oh, it's so hard," I said, thankful she was starting to talk about something that mattered. "But the pain is the same for you with your mom gone. I'm blessed to have my brother Aimable alive in Senegal, and he's going to visit soon, I hope. Two of my aunts and three of my cousins also survived. But my poor Jeanette, you lost everyone. I can't imagine how hard it must be for you. I came to tell you that I'm here for you . . . I'm your family now. I make pretty good money at my job, so we can get a place of our own soon. We can live together like sisters, just as we planned when we were little girls."

"What's that, Imma? Oh no, I don't want to move from here. I'm okay. In fact, I'm better than okay. You should see my new boyfriend—he's so handsome. I'm sure you would be jealous."

"You have a boyfriend?"

"Oh yeah, he's from Zaire. He's so romantic; he really knows how to treat a woman. He's not going to ask me to marry him, but that's fine with me. I just want to have a good time."

My heart sank again as I realized that Jeanette had no interest in talking about our families or our futures. She went on and on about her boyfriend, telling me such intimate details about their relationship that I could feel myself blush. No matter how close we'd once been, the girl I knew would never have revealed such scandalous behavior to me. I tried to change the conversation a dozen times, but Jeanette either couldn't or wouldn't talk about anything else.

I made one last attempt to shake her out of her trauma by reminding her of how devout we'd always been. "Remember how we loved the Blessed Mother so much that we were convinced our prayers would make her appear before us?" I asked. "Why don't we pray together now, like we did when we were kids?"

"I'd like to get my hair done, too . . . my boyfriend would really like it."

I put my arms around Jeanette, kissed her on the forehead, and said, "I must go now, dear, but I'll come back tomorrow and we can talk some more."

Here is a new type of heartache, I realized as I left Jeanette's house. I became tortured by my thoughts: *How many different kinds of sorrow are there in the world? How many are we meant to endure?* I was learning to deal with the pain of having my family taken from me, but they were dead—physically gone—*that* I understood. Now I'd actually found someone I loved and could hold in my arms, yet she wasn't there. How could I lose someone who was sitting right beside me? Jeanette was indeed lost to me; she had died from the inside out. It was all so cruel and unfair that it felt like punishment.

I spent the night in my room at Christus, crying and talking to God. "What great wrong did I do in my past to deserve this?" I asked Him. "What are You trying to teach me with such a painful lesson? Why leave my dear friend but take away our great friendship? Please tell me what You want me to understand by leaving me so lonely. Are You a jealous God? Do You want to keep everyone else away from me so that You will always be the center of my life? I love You, but I need a friend, too!"

A heavy, fresh sadness cloaked me. I knew that the Lord wasn't really punishing me, but He did expect me to learn something from the pain I felt. Perhaps He wanted to give me another lesson in unconditional love by showing me that I must love Jeanette even though she might never love me in return. I swore that I would.

For the rest of that night, I made peace with God. The longer I thought about the unfairness of losing a friend, the more I realized I wasn't blaming Him; I was finding a way to tell Him about my new suffering. This was one of those times Sister Michelle had warned me about in high school, when the only one I'd be able to talk to was God. The world continued to shift around me, the people I loved were taken, and the places I'd loved were changed. God was the only thing that was constant in my life, the only friend Who would never leave—He was my best friend. The more heartache I found, the more I realized that surrendering myself was not a onetime deal; it would be a lifetime commitment.

I closed my eyes and prayed, "Dear Father, please watch over Jeanette and help heal her heart and mind. She was always a faithful handmaiden to You, and she needs Your help now. I need Your help as well, because the pain of losing her friendship is too great. I give the pain to You, Lord—please take it from me."

I woke the next morning feeling so much better than I had the night before, and I set off to see Jeanette right away. She was the same, but this time I didn't ask her to pray with me. I just started praying out loud myself: I asked God to be with us and to help my friend find peace with Him again. We sat together all day . . . and before I left, I braided her hair like mine.

JEANETTE WAS THE FIRST OF MANY RWANDANS I WOULD MEET who'd been pushed to the edge of madness by their emotional wounds. My friend was pretty, she looked healthy, and she could feed herself, which was so much more than tens of thousands of other men and women in our country could hope for. The hospitals were overflowing with the maimed and dismembered and were lucky to find bandages to dress the wounds of severed limbs, let alone get drugs to treat psychiatric problems. There were virtually no nurses or doctors of any kind in the country—certainly no mental-health therapists.

People were starving, living in squalor in vast tent cities that had been set up all over the country. In truth, the camps for these individuals, who were known as "internal refugees," were places of great violence, suffering, rape, and disease. The problems faced by Jeanette and the thousands like her whose minds couldn't deal with the horror didn't even register on the scales of our nation's troubles.

Part of me had been waiting for Jeanette to come back to Rwanda so that I could truly start over as I built a new family with my old friend. But I could see that this was not going to happen. I'd never abandon her, but I knew that our dream of sisterhood was yet another victim of the genocide.

I continued to visit Jeanette over the years and pray beside her. She always knew my name, but she never remembered our bond of friendship. I heard later that after I left Rwanda, she had to be institutionalized. My friend Mary told me that when she last visited her in the hospital, Jeanette was finally getting the medication she needed and her mind had cleared a little.

Mary also said that Jeanette had called out my name during her visit, saying, "Everything will be okay again when Imma gets here! Everything will be okay when we pray together."

I promised myself that the next time I returned to Rwanda, the first thing I would do would be to go to Jeanette and do just that.

CHAPTER 7

EXILES, EXODUS, AND KILLERS ACROSS THE WATER

"Why are you still alive?"

"I beg your pardon?" I asked.

I searched the face of the tall woman standing ahead of me in the UN cafeteria's lunch line. We'd bumped against each other accidentally, and I'd automatically apologized to her in Kinyarwanda.

She looked at me sternly and repeated herself. "I said, 'Why are you still alive?'"

"My name is Immaculée," I responded, too taken aback to actually answer her question.

"Okay . . . Immaculée. So why *are* you still alive?"

"A Hutu pastor hid me and seven other women. God protected us," I answered, noting that this woman was evaluating my every word.

"What about your parents?"

"Both killed."

"Do you have brothers and sisters?"

"I had three brothers, now I have one."

She smiled gently, extended her hand to me, and said, "Hello, Immaculée. I'm Anne, and I'm a Tutsi, too."

That's how my friendship with Anne began. She was a strong-willed woman with a lifelong faith in God and a burning distrust of Hutus everywhere. Anne's parents were "'59ers," the name given to Tutsis who hurriedly fled Rwanda for neighboring countries during the Hutu Revolution that began in 1959. Tens of thousands of Tutsis were killed in that first round of mass murder; and more than 100,000 went into exile in Uganda, Burundi, Tanzania, and Zaire. Yet the forced emigration of 1959 was only the first wave of the Tutsi diaspora. In fact, before the 1994 genocide, hundreds of thousands of Tutsis had left the country in the wake of successive anti-Tutsi pogroms during the preceding decades.

Like so many other Tutsi parents, Anne's mother and father had packed up their lives and their children, choosing to raise their family in exile rather than risk being caught in the next outbreak of deadly ethnic violence. Yet once they'd left, they could never come back.

After the coup of 1973, Tutsis who'd chosen to live in exile were officially banished for life by the Hutu government. Most of the rebel Tutsi army (including its leader, future Rwandan president Paul Kagame), were actually children of exiles and grew up beyond our country's borders. One of the first things the Tutsi rebels did after forming the postholocaust government was to call for all Tutsis who had gone (or been born) into exile over the past 35 years to come home. More than a million Tutsis answered that call, including Anne and her family.

So when my new friend grilled me so brusquely about my background, I understood that she wasn't being intentionally rude. Many members of her family had been butchered, and she, like every survivor in the country, played it safe when it came to strangers.

With the exception of "Hello," the most common greeting in Rwanda was now either "Why are you alive?" or "How did you survive the genocide?"

Although raised in Rwanda's culture of inherent courteousness and habitual good manners, most survivors dispensed with the politeness and went straight for the information they needed in order to sum you up quickly. It wasn't that people had been too brutalized to be friendly, although that was often true, but caution preempted courteousness. It wasn't rudeness; it was a matter of survival.

Tutsis needed to know exactly where people came from as soon as they met them. No one was quite sure who was a murderer and who wasn't, because thousands upon thousands of Hutus had killed someone. Some Tutsis said that the murder of so many men, women, and children by machete in less than 100 days required the active participation of millions of collaborators. The common assumption was that if Hutus hadn't personally killed any Tutsis, then they'd either reported the whereabouts of their Tutsi friends or neighbors or had closed their doors to someone crying out for help. Either way, they'd taken part in the genocide.

In our ruined country, most survivors believed that if you were a Hutu, you were a murderer who would murder again, given the opportunity.

Of course this was far from the truth, as being Hutu did not automatically make a person a killer. Thousands of Hutu moderates had protested the genocide from the start and had been viciously executed as traitors. Those who refused to murder or rape, or didn't cheer on those who did, had been killed as Tutsi sympathizers. And countless men and women, such as the pastor who'd hidden me and the seven other ladies, had risked their lives to help their Tutsi neighbors. Many Hutus were good, kind, and loving people . . . but so many others were guilty of horrendous crimes.

Tutsi survivors needed, wanted, and demanded to find out whose hands were bloody and whose were clean. But it was difficult to know who had killed; it was difficult just knowing if someone was Hutu or Tutsi if you hadn't grown up with him or her. The outdated physical stereotypes that supposedly identified our two tribes were just that—stereotypes.

The truth was, it was hard to tell Hutus or Tutsis apart simply by looking at them, and even if you knew that individuals were Hutu, there was no way of knowing if they'd been involved in the killing unless a witness had been left to tell. But relatively few witnesses had been left alive, and those who had escaped were reluctant to point their fingers at the killers—survivors who accused a Hutu of a crime often wound up dead. It was a fact of life that killers returned to their communities as though nothing had happened, and survivors had to live beside those who had hacked their families to bits.

ON TOP OF THAT, TUTSIS WHO LIVED NEAR THE BORDER OF ZAIRE, such as those in my home village, were threatened nightly by killers who had crossed over into that country to regroup and then snuck back into Rwanda under cover of darkness to take revenge on survivors.

Zaire had become infected with the cruel, homicidal hatred so deeply rooted in the hearts of Rwanda's extremist killers, and the disease began to spread.

Tens of thousands of killers from the Interahamwe militia and the ranks of the Hutu government's army fell back into Zaire as Paul Kagame's RPF troops advanced across Rwanda, fighting to end the genocide. The killers escaped justice by blending in with the Hutu exodus—the mass of humanity that fled Rwanda after the genocide, fearing revenge killings by Tutsi rebels and vengeful survivors.

The number of refugees was almost too large to comprehend: two million Hutus, all afraid for their lives. Their fear was stoked by the retreating killers, who convinced Hutu peasants and farmers that remaining in Rwanda was suicide—Hutu men would be tortured, Hutu boys castrated, and Hutu women and girls raped and mutilated. They created a panic and mass hysteria among ordinary Hutus across the country. When villagers responded to the killers' fearmongering by abandoning their huts and heading for Zaire's border, the Interahamwe followed them at a distance, firing their weapons into the air to dupe the terrorized mob into thinking that merciless Tutsi rebels were right behind them. The killers herded the Hutu crowd together and propelled it forward as though they were managing a cattle drive.

It was like watching a dam burst after a devastating storm,

this flash flood of humans a quarter mile wide and 50 miles long. Hutu fathers, mothers, and children were swept along toward an uncertain future with only the possessions they could carry on their heads or backs to begin a new life.

The killers used the Hutu exodus as a shield as they retreated from the Tutsi rebels, and then as a bargaining tool when they reached Zaire. The organizers of the genocide knew that all of these refugees would elicit a massive humanitarian response from the West, and the killers intended to cash in on the multimillion-dollar programs for aid that would inevitably follow the refugees' trail of suffering.

The great irony was that the West had sat by and done nothing during the Tutsi slaughter yet came to the rescue of the refugees in Zaire. In the eyes of the rest of the world, the fleeing Hutus were the real victims of the genocide. And I suppose that by the time they reached Zaire, they had indeed become victims, as only hardship and horror awaited them.

I CROSSED PATHS WITH THE EXODUS WHILE BEING EVACUATED from the French refugee camp I stayed in after leaving Pastor Murinzi's house. The French had arrived in Rwanda toward the end of the genocide and were welcomed into the country by the Hutu extremist government, who believed that their foreign friends would help them complete the Tutsi extermination. The French had had close ties with the Hutu government for years and had even financed and trained many Hutu soldiers. Tutsis tended to believe that the French had trained Hutu soldiers in the most efficient methods of killing and had provided the extremists enough money to purchase machetes by the ton.

The French and the Tutsi rebel soldiers distrusted each other fiercely, and both sides were under orders to avoid a confrontation that might accidentally trigger an international conflict. The Tutsi rebels didn't cross into the safe zone that the French established, and the French didn't get directly involved in the civil war—or fire a single shot to end the holocaust. The Hutu killers, along with some chief architects of the genocide, took advantage of the situation and marched freely through the French safe zone to reach Zaire. Many people say that the only reason the French came to Rwanda was to create an escape corridor for the killers they had long supported.

Whatever their motives, the French did save the lives of many Tutsis. However, while they protected me when I came out of hiding, I don't owe them for keeping me alive—that sentiment is reserved for God. You see, when the Hutu exodus passed by our refugee camp, the French soldiers loaded 30 of us survivors into the back of a truck, promising to take us to the safety of a Tutsi rebel encampment. Instead, the soldiers abandoned us right in front of a group of Interahamwe. The French deserted me, but the Lord protected me from the killers that night with the absolute power of His love.

As one of the Interahamwe advanced on me with his machete, I prayed for God to enter my soul and let His love pour through my eyes and into the killer's, forcing him to see the evil he was committing. Sure enough, my prayer was answered: With a simple look of love, the man turned his head in shame, dropped his machete, and left me in peace. And when other killers came at me with their blades, God delivered me to the safety of the Tutsi rebel camp. The killers rejoined the exodus and followed it out of the country.

By the time the refugees entered Zaire, the Hutus had run out of food and water and began dying by the thousands—they perished from starvation, exhaustion, and illness. One cholera outbreak alone killed 50,000 Hutus (mostly the children and elderly) in just a few weeks.

As the killers had assumed, the UN and other relief organizations poured millions of dollars in food and supplies into eastern Zaire, where tent cities were built to shelter a refugee population larger than the population of the American state of New Hampshire.

As long as the refugees were there, the money would continue to flow, so the killers made sure that the refugees weren't going anywhere. Hundreds of thousands of Hutus were held as virtual prisoners by the killers, who organized the camps like medieval fiefdoms: They pocketed relief money, stole the refugees' food, raped the women, turned thousands of girls into sex slaves, and murdered anyone who tried to go back to Rwanda.

For Hutu refugees, life in the camps was misery. But the killers prospered. They were well armed, well fed, and plotting to come back to Rwanda to finish the genocide. They formed an insurgent Hutu army, with thousands of soldiers stationed on the other side of the Rwandan border—they believed that when they attacked, the Hutus who had stayed in Rwanda would rise up with them against the Tutsis.

On the other side of Lake Kivu, the killers were preparing a second holocaust. It was a deadly threat that Tutsi survivors lived under every day.

AT THE SAME TIME AS THE HUTU EXODUS OUT OF RWANDA, a great number of the Tutsis who had lived in exile for years—many born and raised in foreign cultures—began pouring into the country from all directions.

For a while, living in Rwanda was like being part of the biblical story of the Tower of Babel: We were all the same tribe, all one people, but we had a lot of trouble understanding each other. For example, Tutsis who had grown up in Zaire arrived in Rwanda speaking a broken Kinyarwanda that was liberally mixed in with the Swahili they'd learned in school. And it wasn't only the words that were different; what they said and the way they said it shocked Rwandan Tutsis.

Zairians spoke their minds openly and voiced their opinions loudly, which went completely against the grain of Rwandan-born Tutsis. We were brought up to talk quietly, thoughtfully, and with deference and courtesy to others; and, above all things, to be modest. Besides being boisterous and forward, Zairians acted very hip and cool in public. They loved pop music, dancing, and wearing fashionable clothes, which was all viewed as being in poor taste in a country where most people were facing starvation. Still, there was an innocence to Zairians, who were open, ready to laugh, and smiled easily—all of which were welcome sights for our war-weary eyes. They were a bright addition to our Tutsi population.

Since Ugandan Tutsis had been raised in a country colonized by the British, they spoke English, as opposed to the French spoken by their Rwandan cousins. Remarkably, the European Franco-Anglo rivalry seemed to flare up between the two groups of Tutsis in our little African nation. The Rwandans thought that the Ugandans were cold and money oriented, and the Ugandans considered the Rwandans to be snobby and foolish. But because Paul Kagame was from Uganda, and Ugandan Tutsis formed the backbone of the rebel army that ended the genocide, every Tutsi in Rwanda considered them heroes and saviors.

Tutsis from Burundi spoke Kirundi, a cousin language to Kinyarwanda that Rwandans could understand when it was spoken slowly . . . but Burundians didn't like doing anything slowly. They tended to be, like my friend Anne, blunt and impatient toward the conservative and deferential nature of Rwandan Tutsis, especially when it came to living with Hutus. Burundi had virtually the same ethnic mix as did Rwanda, about 85 percent Hutu and 14 percent Tutsi (and one percent Twa), but the cultural similarity ended there.

As difficult as it is to understand, despite the frequent outbreaks of mass murder, Hutus and Tutsis in Rwanda actually lived together peacefully on a day-to-day basis. Until the genocide, I felt safe almost everywhere I went in my nation, as people didn't fight each other, there was little violent crime, and everyone was civil. Burundi was altogether different.

My friend Sarah, who is Hutu and lived in Burundi during the genocide, told me that she'd never been more frightened in her life than in that country.

"Immaculée, you know that Hutus and Tutsis got along here in Rwanda, and it was usually peaceful. But in Burundi, I thought I was going to be murdered every time I went out the door," she said. "Everyone—Tutsis and Hutus—walked around with big knives sticking out of their belts and were ready to use them if somebody looked at them the wrong way. You had to be careful where you walked because the two tribes lived in segregated neighborhoods, so take one wrong turn and you could wind up dead. All these Tutsis coming here from Burundi make me really nervous."

Even Anne, who was a gentle person by nature, had no tolerance when it came to Hutus. "We don't put up with being bullied by them," she told me. "I will never understand how you Tutsis in Rwanda sat back and let these Hutu monsters kill everybody. Tutsis here are pacifists and pushovers; they act like born victims. In my country, many Tutsis refuse to turn the other cheek. If a Hutu kills a Tutsi, two Hutus are killed in return. If one of our girls is raped, two of their girls get raped. When they hit us, we hit back."

I knew that Burundian Tutsis were fierce, but they were also proud of their Tutsi heritage and inspired Rwandan Tutsis to embrace and celebrate their culture. So I always said this silent prayer when I heard Burundian Tutsis start talking about Hutus: *God, we've had enough bloodshed between neighbors to last until doomsday. Please don't let new hatred and violence be planted in our soil. Use me to spread Your word and help make peace in our troubled country.*

DESPITE THEIR DIFFERENCES, RETURNING EXILES HAD ALL PLAYED a part in the nation's liberation and were proud to be called Rwandan. And they'd all returned to the country with similar expectations— they'd crossed the border believing Rwanda to be a paradise. Their parents remembered the country's physical beauty, strong familial bonds, and sense of community spirit through the nostalgic eyes of exiles. They passed that vision along to their children, who grew up with a mythical image of Rwanda.

Yet when those children arrived here, they found a country torn apart by war and genocide. Instead of paradise, they came upon a wasteland permeated with death and destruction. The disappointment many newcomers carried around with them was palpable, and it was a disappointment they were always ready to share.

"I left a good government job in Kampala, and I sold everything I had to bring my wife and kids here," complained Laurence, my new Ugandan neighbor who'd moved into an abandoned house near Sarah's. "All my life, my dad told me that Rwanda was like a Garden of Eden—life was easy, and the countryside was the most beautiful in Africa. But I come here and I can't get work, I live in a hovel, and I can't even feed my family. What kind of Eden is this?"

I wanted to tell Laurence that he was lucky, since most Rwandan Tutsis were now either buried in mass graves or living in UN refugee tents drinking dirty water and dying from dysentery. But I never said anything negative to Laurence, or any of the former exiles I met. For some reason, I always felt a little responsible when Tutsis came to my country from outside and were unhappy with it. I suppose it was part of true Rwandan culture, as we were raised to make guests feel welcome, comfortable, and at home.

The clash of cultures between the native Tutsis and the Tutsi returnees often sparked arguments and even physical fights. There were endless misunderstandings, because even when we surmounted the language barrier, there was the body-language barrier—the hand gestures we used, the type of eye contact we made, the way we laughed, and even the way we walked were different for every group, sometimes disturbingly so. We were all related, but we were strangers to each other.

No matter how much confusion arose between the old and new Tutsis of Rwanda, it was all friendly banter compared to the anger and hostility reserved for Hutu refugees who dared return from Zaire.

By the first fall after the genocide, a small but steady stream of these refugees began coming back to our country. Many died while attempting the brutal journey through thick jungles and deep swamps swarming with malaria-carrying mosquitoes, giant crocodiles, and other wild animals; and those who did make it were often portraits of unbelievable misery.

I remember seeing one family stumbling down a road during a visit home to Mataba. There were two boys who may have been 11 or 12, but they were so malnourished, weak, and drawn that they looked like hunched-up old men: Their backs were bent and twisted, their legs were bowed by rickets, and their clothes were filthy rags caked in mud and excrement. The two of them dutifully followed their mother, who trudged on in front of them, her eyes fixed and vacant like a zombie's, her teeth jutting from her tightened lips. In her bent, bony right arm, she dangled the limp body of an infant.

The scene was as horrific as it was familiar—I'd seen Tutsi families crawl out of the bush after three months of hiding much like the poor Hutu wretches walking by me. I offered them some coins, but they passed by without looking at me.

Dear God, I thought, *is this Your punishment against the Hutus? Why these children, Lord? Please ease their suffering. Bring the baby home, and watch over the mom and the little boys.*

I wondered if the boys' father had been a killer, if his sins were now being visited upon his own loved ones. Were the innocent paying for the mindless, thoughtless crimes that had been committed by an earlier generation? This sad, suffering family was a warning to those who acted out of anger and hatred—sin afflicted the innocent and guilty alike.

I walked to my old home, to where Mom and Damascene were buried, and got down on my knees. As they always did at the gravesite, my tears flowed freely, and I prayed, "Please, Lord, move the hearts of the men and women in our new government. Convince our leaders to create a Ministry of Love. What better weapon to protect the world from evil and pain than by arming everyone with words of love?"

Later that day I visited with Angie and Tare, two Tutsi friends who hadn't been in the village during the genocide. Angie was my age and had just moved to Mataba from Burundi, where she'd grown up. I'd known Tare since we were kids, and he'd been a happy child until several of his relatives in Gisenyi province were killed by extremists.

Tare was a little older than I was and had left Mataba before the civil war started in 1990 to join the RPF in Uganda. He'd almost convinced Damascene and Vianney to go off with him, but my mother had suffered an asthma attack when she heard about the attempt to recruit her boys. She made my brothers swear that they'd never join the rebels.

"Look at me. I can hardly breathe. Are you trying kill me?" my mother asked dramatically, clutching her chest. "Are my own sons trying to kill me? Promise me you will never become soldiers and go off to get shot. Promise me!"

The boys knew that Mom was using her health problems to guilt them into staying in school and away from the rebels, but it worked, and they took a solemn oath to stay out of the war. Ironically, if they *had* joined, they may have had a fighting chance to survive.

Anyway, Tare had battled for years against Hutu extremists and the Interahamwe, and he was now very bitter. He'd fought to protect his sisters and mother, but while he was with the army in the north, the Interahamwe had descended upon our village and killed every member of his family.

As the three of us stood chatting in front of Tare's home, we saw an older woman limping up a hill behind the cowshed. She was using a tree branch as a walking stick, her skin was chalky white from the dust, and she had sores all over her face, but I still thought I knew who she was.

"Mushaha, is that you?"

"Bless you for recognizing me, Immaculée! You're the first one who has."

Although Mushaha was a Hutu, she'd been one of my mother's close friends. When I was young and home on school holidays, Mushaha and I would pray together in a little chapel close to our house. And I frequently went swimming with her family in Lake Kivu and kept an eye on her sweet twin children, Jocelyn and François.

I stepped forward to give her a hug, but she backed away, saying, "Thank you for your kindness, but I'm sick. You'd better not touch me."

"What happened to you?" I asked, seeing the pain etched on her diseased face. She was half the size she'd been when we'd last met at a Mass before the genocide. "Where are François and Jocelyn? Where are your husband and parents?"

Mushaha's chin trembled, and tears rolled down her cheeks, cutting dark lines through the dust she wore like a mask. "Oh,

Immaculée," she replied, "they're dead. They're all dead . . . dead in Zaire!"

"Immaculée, come here!" Tare hissed. I took a few steps back to where he and Angie stood, and he angrily asked, "Why are you talking to her? Her husband was a killer, and she laughed when the Tutsis were being slaughtered here. She is dead to us; don't touch her, don't talk to her, don't even look at her. Let the bitch rot."

"Your pity disgusts me," Angie added, almost jumping at me because she was so upset. "How can you stand to touch that pig? There's Tutsi blood on those hands—she told the killers where to find my cousins and caused all this agony. I only wish someone were chasing *her* down with a machete and trying to kill *her*. Then maybe she'd start to feel what it's like. It's their turn to suffer, Immaculée. Let her suffer."

My friends' words, so hateful and harsh, stung my heart. I understood their rage, which came from their grief, but I also knew how much it was harming them. If we were to ever start healing in Rwanda, we'd better start here and now. What better place to begin than with an ailing mother who'd lost her children?

"I know how you feel," I told Tare and Angie, "but we can't hate everybody, or the hatred will never end. This isn't a mob of killers standing at the gate; it's not an entire tribe. She's just one wounded woman, and she's in pain. She needs our help."

Their eyes branded me a traitor and they shook their heads. Then they turned their backs to me and walked into Tare's house without saying good-bye.

I went back and sat on the ground beside Mushaha, who was quietly weeping on the roadside. I held her hand, remembering how she'd comb the water from my hair after swimming, how her children loved to chase my dad's goats, how she'd help my mother sew wedding dresses for young brides in the village, and how she'd always brought our family little gifts after church on Sundays. It was hard for me to imagine her laughing at our neighbors— maybe at my own family—as they were hunted and killed. But the madness, the lust for blood, had made so many good people unbelievably wicked.

What power the devil must wield on Earth to so thoroughly corrupt a gentle soul, I thought. *Of course the only protection from such evil is God's love, the only redemption for those who have lost their way.*

"I'm so sorry for what happened to your mom," Mushaha said through her tears. "Rose was a beautiful woman . . . and your father . . . oh, I don't know what evil overtook our village. I curse everyone who did it. Now we must endure the consequences of our actions . . . we must taste ashes and fire." She began wailing now, swallowing air with labored, wheezing gulps.

"My children are dead, Immaculée!" she cried. "The cholera killed them . . . they died one after the other! They died in my arms, looking into my eyes. What kind of mother am I? How could I take my little darlings into such a hell? The Interahamwe stole all our food, I had nothing to give my babies to eat, no water to put on their bleeding lips! The Interahamwe forced us to move, saying that the Tutsis were coming to kill us. They made us march day and night through the jungle. We walked and walked and walked for weeks. The children's shoes fell apart, and their feet got so infected that every step made them scream. But they kept forcing us to walk."

She took a second to try to calm down, and then continued, "After a few weeks the ground started shaking under us, and a volcano exploded. Ash and fire fell on us, the air was like hot poison . . . it was God striking us down. It was like the world was ending, and He was delivering His vengeance upon us. The smoke was so thick that I couldn't see and the children couldn't breathe. My husband fell down coughing and never got up.

"We ran into a swamp and stayed there for two days, and that's when the sickness found us. People just fell down dead. Over a thousand people died in one day. I had to sit on top of the dead bodies to hold my babies above the muck. The stink and the flies, and the thirst . . . it *was* hell. My babies died in my arms, and I had to leave them lying on top of the corpses of strangers. Immaculée, God has forsaken us . . . He has forsaken me. Why didn't I die with my children?"

My heart ached for this woman, and I asked God to make a special place for François and Jocelyn in heaven. Mushaha's story made me see how the devil had used the genocide to bring suffering and sorrow to Hutus and Tutsis alike. Satan didn't choose sides—he was the enemy of all humankind.

"God hasn't forsaken you," I told her. "He forsakes no one. But you must open your heart to Him and ask for His forgiveness. If you've committed crimes here in the village, you'll have to answer to the village, but only God knows your heart and what's in it. You must let Him into your soul and ask Him to heal you with His love."

"I will, but my sins are so terrible. I let my children die and left them to rot . . . are their souls in hell? Are my babies in hell?"

"Your children are with God, and heaven is a much better place than where they were. They're happy with Jesus, who takes care of children. I will pray for them, Mushaha, but you'll have to find God on your own. You won't be able to forgive yourself without His love."

"Thank you, Immaculée. Please pray for me and for all of us sinners. Our hatred has destroyed us."

I helped her to her feet, gave her what little money I had, and hugged her good-bye.

As Mushaha struggled on her way with her tree branch, I wondered what plan God had to restore love to our battered homeland. I thought about the Hutu refugees dying in Zaire and of the silent mother carrying her dead baby to a home that no longer existed. I thought about the disappointment and anger of the returning Tutsi exiles, and I thought of the heartache carried by everyone.

Dear Lord, please send us a miracle to bring us back together. Make us one people, one family that can love each other and live as You intended us to live. Please, God, Rwanda needs Your help.

In the coming years, I believe that God answered this prayer through President Paul Kagame, who abolished the tribal identity cards that separated and divided Rwandans for so many generations. One of the happiest days of my life was when he made a speech in which he proclaimed that from that day forward, no one in the country would ever again be referred to as Hutu, Tutsi, or Twa.

"From now on," he promised, "there will be no more tribes. We are one family; we are all Rwandans."

I had faith that God would make President Kagame's words Rwanda's reality.

CHAPTER 8

LOOKING FOR MIRACLES

"Damascene, is it you? Are you alive?"

The man in front of me raised his arms to protect his face, thinking that a crazy woman was about to attack him.

"I'm sorry, sir. I'm so sorry," I mumbled, before quickly turning away and hurrying down the street. But at the next corner, it happened again: a powerful flash of recognition, an almost painful jolt of joy, and an uncontrollable physical reaction.

"Wait!" I shouted, running up behind another man, grabbing him by the shoulders, and spinning him around to face me.

Damascene, is it you? It is you! Oh, you are alive! my mind reeled. Then, once again, my sweeping emotional letdown was followed by an embarrassed apology to a startled stranger.

For the first time in my life, I was outside of Rwanda, and I was feeling quite lost. I'd traveled to Nairobi, the capital city of Kenya, to apply for a visa to go to Canada after a friend at the UN asked a relative to sponsor me. I didn't even know where Canada was, but it sounded far away and like a good place to start over.

Because consulates in Rwanda were still closed, thanks to the genocide, I made the 24-hour bus trip to Nairobi to get to the nearest Canadian embassy. As soon as I stepped off the bus, the noise, heat, and crowds overwhelmed me—I couldn't take a step without being knocked into by someone. The roads were jammed with taxis, minivans, and buses; huge planes roared overhead; the high-pitched buzzing of a hundred motorbikes enveloped me; and the thick, hazy fumes in the air made my lungs burn and my eyes water. It was unlike any place I had ever been.

Before I'd boarded the bus in Kigali, I'd been warned that a lot of people lived in Nairobi, but nothing could have prepared me for what I found. I wouldn't have believed such a place existed; after all, how could I have pictured what two million people would look like? All of them crammed together and yet somehow managing to walk in different directions? *Two million people!* It seemed impossible for so many to gather in one place at one time—God must have assembled them here for some reason.

Maybe it was the strain of being trapped in an airless bus for an entire day and night, all of the disturbing images I'd witnessed in the destroyed villages I passed while traveling out of Rwanda, or the anxiety of leaving my homeland for the first time. Whatever the reason, as soon as I walked out of the bus depot, my mind started playing tricks on me. I somehow decided that Nairobi was a part of heaven, so it made perfect sense that my parents and brothers were walking around somewhere in the crowd. All I had to do was look carefully enough and I'd spot them. And sure enough, I *did* see them. The faces of each of my departed family members appeared amidst the throng of people streaming around me beneath the blazing Kenyan sun. Within an hour I'd accosted at least four young men, all of whom I'd convinced myself were Damascene.

"You did what?" my friend Dorothée asked, giggling at me as I arrived at the small second-floor room where she lived with her sweet little daughter, Liberate. "They will lock you up, Immaculée. You can't walk around the streets of Nairobi acting completely mad. And you definitely can't go around grabbing strange men!"

"I know, Dorothée, I know," I replied, chuckling at myself. "But I *swear* I saw them all out there in the crowd . . . at least, I saw

Damascene for sure." I looked down at the bustling street from her window. "There are so many people that my parents and brothers *must* be here. How could they not be?"

Dorothée had escaped to Kenya through Tanzania after the genocide started, but not before her brothers and father had been murdered. She ran for Rwanda's border, carrying her baby in her arms, and managed to hike across Tanzania and reach her relatives in Nairobi. She'd developed a no-nonsense outlook on life and was unimpressed by, and dismissive of, my conviction that my family members had somehow risen from the dead and were alive and well and wandering the streets of her city.

"Immaculée, you buried your mother and Damascene yourself, and you know that Vianney and your father are dead. What are you talking about?"

"I know it sounds insane, but I can't shake the feeling that they're here. You know, I never saw the bodies of Dad or Vianney, and Mom and Damascene were just bones when I buried them . . . so technically, there's a chance that they're still alive."

"You're nuts," my friend said, shaking her head at me. But after I'd insisted with such certainty for more than an hour, Dorothée started to wonder if there was something to what I said.

"You must be making me nuts as well," she told me. "But if your family is alive, then *mine* probably is, too!" She gathered Liberate into her arms, and the three of us descended into the streets of Nairobi to search for our loved ones. We stopped maybe a dozen people, quite sure they belonged to us, but of course they did not. After several hours, we returned to Dorothée's room. Exhausted, we collapsed on her bed amid tears and peals of laughter at how utterly silly we'd been. We laughed until our faces hurt.

"Immaculée, look out the window—do you really think that there's air pollution in heaven?"

Dorothée and I teased each other about our misadventure for the rest of that week I stayed with her. My visa application for Canada was rejected, but my trip to Nairobi boosted my spirits and showed me that God finds many ways to tickle us, even in the depths of despair. I also learned that when we have suffered a loss too great to bear, our hearts and minds are open to miracles . . . and sometimes even a little miracle can sustain our faith and help us survive.

ONE MIRACLE STORY THAT SPREAD ACROSS RWANDA after the holocaust was that of a four-year-old girl named Mimi. I heard the tale from my friend Lilly, who heard it from her Presbyterian minister, who heard it from a Hutu prisoner who claimed to be an eyewitness. Whatever its origins, it spread so fast among Rwandans that it was difficult to find anyone who hadn't heard it, and just as difficult— as incredible as it sounds—to find someone who didn't believe it to be true.

As the story goes, Mimi lived in a remote village in a forested region along the Akagera River near Tanzania. When the Interahamwe arrived at her home, Mimi made a life-or-death dash to the forest with her parents and siblings, as well as hundreds of her Tutsi neighbors. But Mimi couldn't keep up with the others and fell behind. She was hiding beneath some bushes and praying to God to save her when the killers found her. One of them held her down while the others started torturing her with their spears, when all of a sudden, a lioness sprang from the forest. She roared ferociously and advanced on the men, who ran away in fear.

When the killers came back for Mimi later, they were met again by the roaring lioness, and again they ran away. For the next three months, the lioness stayed close to Mimi, not only protecting her from the killers, but also feeding her with bananas and meat she carried from the forest in her mouth. When the genocide ended, Mimi's parents came searching for her and saw the lioness stretched out in front of their daughter. This time the beast didn't roar; she walked quietly into the forest and vanished from sight.

Most people who heard the story of Mimi believed the lioness to be an angel of God taking the form of a mighty animal to protect one of His weakest children. Yet many wondered why the Lord would come to Earth as an animal and then save only one little girl—why wouldn't He save all the children?

I think only God knows the answer to this, and maybe we're not meant to know. But I believe in Mimi's tale, and even if it isn't true, it seems that Rwandans love telling it time and again because its simple message resonates with holocaust survivors: No matter how hopeless a life may become, God can use His power to love and protect His most vulnerable children.

ANOTHER MIRACLE STORY THAT BECAME FAMOUS IN MY COUNTRY was that of Leo and his family. Leo was a Tutsi farmer with a devoted wife and eight children, and they were all born-again Christians who prayed together in the evenings and had a deep faith. Two months before the genocide, Leo was in his field gathering sweet potatoes when he received a message from God. He saw a bright light in front of him and heard a voice telling him to stop work, leave his crops, and spend the next two months praying and fasting with his family.

"Pray the evil wind that will soon blow across this land will not stay," the voice said. When Leo returned to his hut, he learned that everyone in his family had received a similar message. For two months, the ten members of Leo's family lived only on water, a single handful of cassava beans in the evening, and prayer. They became the joke of their community: Men dropped by Leo's hut to laugh at the clan who prayed morning, noon, and night while crows ate their crops.

Nevertheless, the family prayed through February, and then through March. They kept praying until the killers reached their village during the rains of April, when the holocaust began. All of Leo's Tutsi neighbors were running for their lives, but he and his family came out of their hut and, with smiles on their faces, calmly greeted the killers.

"It's the family who likes praying so much that they forgot to run away when they had a chance. Do you want to die with that stupid smile on your face?" one of the murderers asked Leo.

"God has ordered us to pray that this evil will be overcome by the hearts of men," the farmer replied. "We have done what He asked and will go to heaven this very day. You may take our bodies but not our spirits. I pity you for the evil you have taken into your soul—your darkness blinds you to God."

And with that, the entire family fell down dead before the killers had a chance to touch them. Most of the murderers believed that they'd witnessed a miracle and dropped their machetes, begged the Lord for forgiveness, and never took another life. But others, who said that Leo and his family had starved themselves to death, went on killing until they had no one left to kill.

A THIRD MIRACLE STORY, WHICH IS OF DIVINE INTERVENTION, is frequently used by Rwandan pastors and priests to encourage people to pray.

Karoli was a major in the RPF, the Tutsi rebel army that toppled the extremist Hutu government and ended the genocide. Afterward, he was put in charge of security for the northwestern province of Gisenyi, where I had gone to high school.

Gisenyi, which borders Zaire, was heavily populated by extremist Hutus and holocaust supporters. Groups of Interahamwe, who'd escaped into Zaire's deep forests after the genocide, would often slip back into Rwanda at night and kill Tutsi families. Hundreds of innocent people continued to be murdered in Gisenyi, so it was a very dangerous place to live if you were Tutsi. Major Karoli and his men were continually kept on their toes by all of the activity.

Because many churches had been destroyed, people often gathered at each other's homes or in open spaces to worship and pray. This worried and infuriated Karoli because most of those worshippers were Hutu, and he suspected that their prayer gatherings were really political meetings. He drove from village to village with his soldiers, who fired their machine guns over the heads of Hutus meeting in groups of three or more or even shot the church steeples where the faithful were praying. The terrorized men and women always scattered, abandoning their prayers.

Karoli said that if Hutus were allowed to assemble, even if they really were praising God, they'd end up plotting against their Tutsi neighbors and plan another genocide. "If they carry Bibles together today, they'll carry machetes together tomorrow," he claimed.

The only thing the major distrusted more than Hutus was prayer. Like many Tutsi soldiers, he had seen so much evil that his heart had turned away from God.

One day Karoli was in a tavern drinking banana beer with his bodyguards when a frightened young man approached him. "I'm sorry to disturb you, sir, and under normal circumstances I would never dare say what I'm about to, but I have a message for you," the lad told the major. "You see, God spoke to me last night in a dream and told me to come to this tavern and tell you that you must stop shooting at people who are praying to Him. I have come to the tavern, and here you are, sir. The dream was so real that I had to tell you . . . it's God's will that you let the people worship."

"Why are you telling me how to do my job? Are you an insurgent?" Karoli asked. "Are you working with the Interahamwe?" He slapped the boy with his right hand, and then he told his guards to take him outside and shut him up. The guards carried out the major's orders, beating up the young man before imprisoning him.

Karoli didn't take what the messenger had said to heart. Although he never killed anyone in the process, he continued to break up Hutu prayer meetings with machine-gun fire.

Two weeks later, an older man walked up to the major and said, "Sir, God instructed me in my sleep to tell you to stop persecuting people who are praying to Him. He said that you should investigate more thoroughly before you break up a prayer meeting, since the people you're scaring away are offering their love to Him."

"So, God speaks to you, does he?" Karoli snapped.

"No, sir, it was only this one time, but He was very clear. He said to tell you, 'I am the protector of my flock and will not tolerate your persecution of the faithful.'"

Karoli struck the man with his right hand and ordered that he be beaten up and thrown in jail with the other messenger. "Let's see how well you can hear God from a prison cell!" he shouted, as his soldiers took the man away.

The next day Karoli received a third visit, this time from a very old woman who came to see him at his barracks. "God told me to tell you to stop persecuting His children," she said. In Rwanda, there is great respect for elders and for women, so Karoli couldn't bring himself to harm the old lady. He thanked her for her visit and had her escorted from the premises.

That night the major fell asleep in his living room while listening to the radio. He'd only been asleep a short while when a voice proclaimed, "Karoli, your heart is hard, and set against Me. I have warned you not to persecute those who pray to Me, but you have ignored My messages. Now I will make you hear. You must learn that God loves and protects His children, Karoli. They are My loved ones, and I am their God. You hear My voice now, but still, you do not listen. Tomorrow, at exactly 6 P.M., I will make you listen; I will show you I am your God as well."

Major Karoli woke with a start. While he'd heard the voice, he refused to believe that it was God's. He called his men and had them search his home for Hutu insurgents who might be playing tricks on him, but his soldiers found no signs that anyone had been near his home. Karoli dismissed the voice, finally deciding that it must have been the radio.

Fearing ridicule from his underlings, the major kept his dream to himself. Even so, he took precautions and had sentinels posted around his house the next day. To make sure he wasn't alone, he hosted a barbecue and invited all his friends. But as the afternoon wore on, he became increasingly agitated—he'd faced death without fear many times during his years as a soldier, but now he felt like a frightened schoolboy about to be caned.

At the appointed hour of 6 P.M., the sky darkened, and a powerful wind descended upon Karoli's house. His friends and soldiers fell to the ground to protect themselves, but the major stood his ground, wrapping his arms around a tree so as not to be blown away. As the wind screeched past him, the major felt a searing pain in his right arm.

The storm ended as abruptly as it had begun, and Karoli looked at his arm. To his horror, he found that his right hand had been completely severed by a piece of flying debris. He didn't seem fazed by the pain; rather, he held his arm high, shook his stump at the sky, and screamed, "Imana intwaye ukuboko yo kabura inka!" Translated literally, it means "God took my hand; may He never own a cow!" In our country, where cows have always been prized above all other possessions, this is the worst curse you could wish upon someone.

The major's friends and soldiers all witnessed the bizarre event, and a few of them rushed him to the hospital. Remarkably, his arm wasn't bleeding when they arrived—scar tissue had formed instantaneously over the cut. The doctor who treated him said that he'd never seen a wound like it before.

Karoli's anger subsided and he repented, quickly becoming devoted to God and prayer. He studied the Bible daily; after several months, instead of breaking up prayer meetings, he began to lead them. He resigned from the army and was soon known throughout the country as one of Rwanda's leading Bible scholars, as well as an impassioned preacher.

I love the story of Major Karoli because it reveals how God takes care of those who worship Him and will use someone who persecutes the faithful to become the greatest advocate for them. Like Saul on the road to Damascus, Karoli needed to witness God's power firsthand before he would convert. The conversion of a persecutor also sends a very strong message, one that has inspired me and thousands of others for centuries: no matter what religion we are, prayer is a powerful and sacred communication between our Father and ourselves, and it must be respected.

MY FRIEND LEONA TOLD ME ABOUT A MIRACLE LIKE KAROLI'S, which turned her brother's vicious hatred to loving forgiveness overnight.

Despite being a born-again Christian, Etienne despised all Hutus. "I have an understanding with God," he said. "I'll love and honor Him and keep His commandments, as long as He understands that I'll always hate the Hutus."

His sister reminded him that their mother was born Hutu, that they had Hutu blood in their veins, and that many Hutus died trying to stop the genocide, including an entire family who offered to shelter their cousins.

"I don't care, Leona," he retorted. "A few good deeds don't make up for a million murders. I will never forgive them, and I don't think God will, either. As far as I'm concerned, all Hutus can go straight to hell."

Etienne and Leona had recently returned with their parents from the neighboring country of Burundi, where they'd waited out the holocaust with relatives who'd fled Rwanda during the 1973 coup. Etienne and Leona had been lucky to get out of the country, but when they came home, they learned that their extended family hadn't been so lucky: Two of their brothers—and every single one of their aunts, uncles, and cousins—had been murdered.

Although all of Etienne's family had been very devout Christians and considered forgiveness among the greatest of virtues, he wore his pain and anger like a crucifix. After his sister reminded him that Jesus told us to turn the other cheek to evil people, I heard him tell her, "Read Deuteronomy 19:21, Leona: 'Show no pity: life for life, eye for eye, tooth for tooth, hand for hand, foot for foot.' I have no pity. I follow the law of retribution, not the rule of forgiveness."

But one night, God sent this young man a dream that changed his life.

Etienne dreamed that he was in the Interahamwe. His face and clothes were covered in blood, and no matter how hard he tried, he couldn't shake a bloody machete from his hand. The weapon was so heavy that his arm felt as if it were being pulled out of its socket. Everywhere he went, people recognized him for the killer he was and hated him with a vengeance. No matter where he turned, he was surrounded by the families of people he'd murdered. There were hundreds of them, moving toward him with their arms outstretched and their fingers pointing at his chest. They repeated one word in unison—a word that echoed around him like an eerie heartbeat: "Killer, killer, killer, killer."

Etienne ran and ran and ran, but he couldn't distance himself from his victims' families. He tried to dig a hole to hide in, but his machete kept cutting into his arms. He recoiled when the hands of his victims pushed through from below the earth and grabbed at him. When he fled to a church to beg God's forgiveness, he couldn't open the door, and he realized that he himself had nailed it shut. Suddenly the church was on fire, and he could hear the screams of children inside—all of them calling out his name. He covered his ears and turned around, only to be confronted by the children's parents and their pointing fingers, along with the chant of "Killer, killer, killer."

There was no compassion to be found for Etienne: his neighbors hated him, God hated him, and he hated himself. In desperation, he ran to a cliff at the edge of Lake Kivu and tried to throw himself off, but his feet stuck fast to the rock. Below him was the water; behind him were his crimes.

He woke up drenched in sweat, and he shouted for joy when he realized that he'd only been dreaming. It wasn't true—he wasn't a killer! He ran to his parents and sister and hugged them. "Thank God I'm not Interahamwe! Thank God I'm not a killer!" he cried out. Etienne immediately got on his knees and asked God to forgive him for hating Hutus. "Please, God, help the killers find peace within their hearts," he prayed. "Help them come to terms with their own dark sins, and find the courage to face You with the truth."

After that dream, Etienne started telling other Tutsis that instead of hating or cursing the Hutus who had committed such unspeakable acts, they should pity them for what they'd done to themselves. He always agreed that the killers should be brought to justice, but he never hesitated to visit the convicted in prison and talk to them about the power of God's forgiveness.

Like Etienne, I didn't believe in avoiding truth or justice. There's been horrendous crime and there must be punishment, yet we will never heal as individuals, or as a nation, until we can forgive each other and start forgiving ourselves. As the Bible tells us, it's best if we shepherd our hearts and give them love; we can leave vengeance to our Lord.

FINALLY, HERE'S A MORE LIGHTHEARTED MIRACLE STORY, which I often share with people when I talk about the power of prayer.

Chinaza and her husband, Kelechi, were Protestant missionaries who devoted much of their time to working with poor churches across Africa. The young Nigerian couple did a lot of volunteer work for the United Nations, and we became good friends, often having long talks about how God made things happen in our lives when we used the power of prayer.

When Chinaza and Kelechi discovered that they were going to have their first child, they moved back to Nigeria, but before they left, they made me promise to come to their home in the city of Lagos for the baby's christening. Six months later, I received a letter enclosing a picture of a beautiful little girl named Abebi, along with a plane ticket.

To get into Nigeria, I first had to get my passport stamped with a visa at the embassy in Nairobi. I arranged an overnight stopover for a Thursday evening so that I could get the visa on Friday. I then planned to fly to Lagos on Saturday and have time to spare before the Sunday christening. I had enough money to stay in a very inexpensive room for one night, buy a bit of food, and take a taxi to the airport.

Everything was fine until I got to the embassy in Nairobi on Friday morning.

"Sorry, the visa officer has been called away on a mission," the woman at the counter told me. "Come back next week."

"But I leave tomorrow!" I cried, in a panic. "My plane ticket will expire, I have no money for a room or food, and I'm expected at a christening in Lagos on Sunday!"

"You have a lot of problems, but you're not going to get a visa," the woman said rudely. "The office is closed until next week, so come back then or go back to where you came from."

I sat down on a bench in the waiting room, took out my father's rosary, and surrendered the matter to God. I silently told Him, *Well, Lord, I need a miracle. You say in the Bible that all things are possible for those who believe. I believe You want me to be there for Abebi's christening, so I'm leaving this to You. I believe in You completely, and I believe that this visa will be stamped. Thank You so much for making it happen.*

After praying for a few hours, I opened my passport, half expecting to see the visa stamp. It wasn't there yet, but I knew that it soon would be, so I sat and waited for the miracle to happen. While I was waiting, I did everything I could to stack the odds in my favor, beginning with filling my heart with forgiveness. I held my rosary and prayed for all the people who had trespassed against me, forgiving each one by name. Then I prayed for forgiveness for anyone I had trespassed against, and mentioned all of them by name.

By then it was noon. I opened my passport and looked for the visa, which wasn't there yet.

The woman from the counter walked by and asked, "What are you still doing here? I told you the visa office is closed, and it's not going to open just because you sit here all day."

"Yes, I understand," I replied. "Do you mind if I sit here anyway?" I knew that if I had faith, it would only be a little longer before I had the visa.

"Suit yourself, but you're not getting a visa. It's impossible. No one is authorized to do it, and the office is closed," the woman answered with finality, leaving me alone in the room.

While I continued to wait for God to show up, I kept on cleaning my heart and praying the rosary to pass the time. After I'd forgiven as many people as I could think of, I repeated all the names again—but this time I sent a prayer and a blessing to each one. Then I thought of each blessing and gift God had given me over the past two years, and thanked Him for each one individually.

"I'm sorry, miss, but we're closing the office for the weekend," the woman at the counter called out to me, but with much more kindness this time. "I'm afraid I'll have to ask you to leave and come back next week."

I opened my passport and looked for the stamped visa, absolutely certain that by now God had taken care of it. But it still wasn't there.

"Oh, I'm sorry," I told the woman, who was now looking at me sympathetically. "I'll leave now."

As soon as I was outside the embassy building, I sat down on a bench and opened my passport again. No visa!

God, what's going on? The embassy is closing. How long do You want me to wait?

I knew that with a little bit of faith, we could move mountains, so I waited for a mountain to come. God would deliver if I continued to believe—the choice was mine to either have faith or give up. I chose faith.

I looked at the birds flying in the sky, I looked at the trees and the sun, and I looked at the flowers in the garden. In that instant,

I realized that there were more beautiful things God had put into the world that I could thank Him for while I waited. I began thanking Him for the clouds, the sky, the humidity, the crickets . . . and anything else I could see, hear, or feel.

It was getting dark, and God still hadn't put a stamp in my passport. *I'm not doubting that You are going to do this, God. But I guess I'll have to ask You to hurry it along a bit. Can we make a deadline for this visa—let's say, 7 P.M.?*

At 6:45, a window in the embassy slid open, and the woman who had been rude to me stuck her head out and waved me over. "I couldn't believe it when I looked outside and saw you sitting there. Please give me the name and address of the people you're visiting in Lagos," she said rather nicely.

Twenty minutes later, a car pulled up in front of the embassy, and the driver jumped out and opened the rear door. "Are you here trying to get a visa?" asked the tall, official-looking man who climbed out.

"Yes, sir."

"Follow me."

A few minutes later, I was back in the embassy, but this time I watched the man place my passport on his desk and stamp it with a visa for Nigeria.

"My assistant doesn't do people favors, so I don't know what kind of magic you worked on her, but she pestered me with phone calls until I drove all the way down here to see you," the man, who turned out to be the visa officer, explained. "You've got to tell me why you waited all day. What made you so certain that you could get a visa when the office was closed?"

"God," I said, with a smile. "I believed that He would make a miracle happen for me, and He did. All I had to do was have faith and patience."

CHAPTER 9

A DREAM
COMES TRUE

One truly great miracle that God performed in my life was leading me to a job at the United Nations headquarters in Kigali.

For a Rwandan, finding any kind of work after the genocide was virtually impossible. Soon after the extremist Hutu government unleashed the holocaust, it shut down the country for business. Hutu government officials even went on the radio to order all citizens to stop work and increase the murder rate: "Your business is killing Tutsis; there will be no other work until the job is done and all the Tutsi cockroaches are dead."

Banks, markets, and shops of every kind closed. Farmers were called away from their fields and handed weapons, schoolboys were pulled out of class and armed with machetes, and trash removers became corpse collectors. The economy shifted overnight from agriculture and commerce to murder and rape.

As it left the capital city, the Hutu army scuttled any chance for even a modest economic recovery by burning financial records, destroying government documents, and completely sacking Kigali. They stole everything they could, from computers to bathroom fixtures, packing it all into military buses and shipping it off to

Zaire, where the killers had regrouped. Before they pulled out, they cut the power lines, contaminated the water supply, torched schools and hospitals, and bombed bridges and roads. They even poisoned the emergency seed supply to destroy the next year's harvest.

Nothing was left behind to help the new Tutsi government fend for itself or feed the starving survivors. UN refugee buses picked up thousands of homeless people from the streets, dropping them off at overflowing refugee camps set up across the country. The camps were never far from my mind because everyone I knew worried about ending up in one, which is what had happened to much of my surviving family.

Nearly all of my cousins, uncles, and aunts had been killed. Miraculously, though, I stumbled upon five of my relatives in the French camp after I'd left the pastor's: two of my mother's sisters, Esperance and Jeanne; and Jeanne's three teenage girls, Consolee, Chantal, and Stella. Jeanne's husband and three sons had been murdered, Esperance's entire family had been exterminated, and my young cousins had suffered unspeakable abuse at the hands of Hutu soldiers.

The five of them had managed to escape into the forest and live alone in the deep woods for three months, surviving on grubs, leaves, and bark. By the time I was reunited with them, they were near death—starving, covered in boils and open sores, lethargic to the point of being comatose, and wearing clothing so ripped and rotten it scarcely covered their nakedness.

While I'd gone to Kigali after the genocide, my aunts and cousins had remained in Kibuye province and faced great difficulty trying to survive. Esperance had been a homemaker and hospital worker, but she no longer had a home to tend, and the hospitals had been destroyed. Jeanne had been a teacher, but the schools were in ruins, and her students were either dead or had fled. Both women were penniless and jobless, and they had three teenage girls to feed . . . there was nowhere for them to go but a refugee camp.

It was difficult to travel anywhere in Rwanda without seeing these camps, which looked like a sea of dark brown or blue tent tops rolling across a hillside or blanketing a valley floor. And tens of thousands of refugees whose homes had been burned down, or who'd had to run away to hide, were existing on occasional packages of dehydrated food while living in a field of foul-smelling muck encircled by trenches of human waste.

The camps were filthy and rife with disease and danger; vile, violent places where rape and murder were commonplace and sickness spread like wildfire. Tutsi survivors suffered the added indignity of living among scores of Interahamwe killers who were pretending to be victims themselves. Yet sadly, for most refugees, living in these shelters was better than the alternative of homelessness and starvation.

My aunts and the girls were in one of the largest, most overcrowded camps in the country, by the town of Gitarama. There was no way I could let my mother's sisters and my vulnerable young cousins languish in such a nasty world. But without having a job myself, there was also no way I could help them, except with my prayers.

MY LIFE IN KIGALI WAS SO MUCH BETTER than what most Rwandans were dealing with. God had truly blessed me, for while I was in the French refugee camp, I'd been "adopted" by a big, boisterous, kindhearted woman named Aloise. Although stricken by polio as a child and confined to a wheelchair for most of her life, Aloise had become an extremely successful woman by catering to the business needs of foreign ambassadors and government officials. She owed her success to a good education, which had been paid for in large part by my mother, who'd been impressed with Aloise's determination in school and wanted to help her.

"Your mother saved my life," Aloise told me when we were introduced. "Rose was an angel to me. If she hadn't helped pay for my schooling, I never would have graduated."

I hadn't known what my mother had done for Aloise, but it didn't surprise me. My parents had put many underprivileged local children through school and had spent much of their salary assisting other people, even when their own family was in need.

Losing the use of her legs hadn't stunted Aloise's growth or personality—she weighed more than 200 pounds and had a big voice and hearty laugh that seemed to echo for miles. "I'll always be grateful to your mom, Immaculée. She was a saint!" she shouted for all the French camp to hear. "I'm going to repay her by helping you!" So she invited me, and eight of the friends I'd made at the camp, to live with her, her husband, and their two small children at the Kigali home they'd fled during the genocide.

I had few options at the time, so I accepted Aloise's offer with thanks. We were lucky enough to then meet a high-ranking officer in the Tutsi rebel army who not only drove us all the way to Kigali, but also supplied us with enough provisions to last for weeks.

Aloise's home was a great, raucous circus, with more than a dozen people scrambling for space in her two-room house. We slept on the floor, washed in the yard, and were coming and going all day long searching for any job to keep us out of a refugee camp.

While hiding in Pastor Murinzi's bathroom, I'd actually had a vision that one day I'd work at the United Nations, where a new and wider world would open up for me. I even borrowed a few English books from the pastor so that I could study the language I'd need to speak when I started my new job.

When I arrived in Kigali, I was confident that I was functionally fluent in English. Of course I'd never actually talked to anyone who spoke it, so I was surprised that no one understood a word I said when I turned up at the UN looking for employment. My smattering of English couldn't get me through the security gate, never mind into the personnel office, so I had to leave my job application with a guard at the door. After several frustrating weeks, I grew discouraged and worried that I might have to give up on my UN dream, but Aloise said something that spurred me on.

It happened on a Monday morning, as I prepared to drop off yet another UN job application. Aloise noticed me standing in front of a jagged shard of mirror, trying in vain to make my survivor clothing look presentable.

"Tsk-tsk," she clucked at me, "why are you wasting your time? There are no jobs for Rwandan women out there, especially for orphans with no friends or family connections." Aloise could be generous to a fault and had a caring soul, but she had also been a survivor all her life and had developed a painfully practical business sense about earning a living.

"Look at yourself, Immaculée: You're wearing rags, your hair is a mess, and you can't speak English. What do you think they see when you show up outside the UN looking for a job? They see a beggar! An illiterate beggar who can't even prove she went to high school or university. You'll never work at the UN . . . but I could get you work *and* lots of money."

She looked me over for a minute and continued, "You're still nice and skinny from not eating for months—foreign men love that look, and they'll pay for it. With my contacts, I'd be able to hook you up with a rich African diplomat, maybe even a white man. We could marry you off temporarily, say for a month or two, and take his money and split it between us. Then I'd find another rich man, and we'd do the same thing again. We could keep it going for years. It would be a great business. Think of all the money we could make!"

I stood there with my mouth open, unable to think of a single word to say.

Aloise's guffaws rang through the house. "Look at your face! You're scandalized, Immaculée! I'm kidding, you know!"

Her words *had* scandalized me. Nobody had ever uttered anything as shocking to me in my life. And as hard as she was laughing, I was sure that she wasn't completely joking.

"Poor dear," Aloise said, catching her breath. "You have no idea how the world works, do you? If you've got something to sell in this life, you'd better do it while you can. You are just too innocent; I don't know how you've made it this far!" Her booming laughter poured from her again.

"Oh, come on, Immaculée. You know I'm only teasing!" She spun her wheelchair around and started to roll down the hall, but before disappearing, she turned and commented, "Think it over, though, because we really would make a lot of money." She gave me a lewd wink and then pushed herself into her room.

Looking in the mirror, I saw what Aloise meant. My clothes *were* in tatters; I was wearing the same outfit I had on when I'd gone into hiding six months before. The slacks and top were worn nearly threadbare from use and repeated scrubbing. My face was still gaunt, and I hadn't had my hair done properly since before the genocide. But I was completely broke! There was so much I needed to do to make myself presentable for a job interview, yet I couldn't afford to do any of it. Without work, I'd end up in the refugee camp with my aunts and cousins . . . and I already looked the part. I left the house and began walking toward the UN. Where else did I have to go?

As I WALKED THROUGH THE STREETS, Aloise's words turned in my mind. I couldn't be angry with her, no matter what she did. She was a good person at heart and had put a roof over my head when I most needed one. But her crass suggestion deeply troubled me, and I wondered what kind of country would arise from the ashes of the holocaust if people were so ready to cash in their morals to survive. If someone had suggested six months before that I sell my body for sex, well . . . it's the kind of thing I never would have heard anyone say.

Even though she was half joking, Aloise had given me a glimpse of the kind of place Rwanda could easily become. I worried that people who'd lost their families and homes wouldn't be able to hold on to their faith. How could true values exist in a land wet with the blood of more than a million people, where tens of thousands were homeless and hungry?

Once again, I despaired for my people and our future. And then I heard a familiar voice in my mind: *Give it up, Immaculée. What's the use? You'll never find work; you're going to end up living in a filthy camp. Why not listen to Aloise? Life would be so easy . . . you could save your aunts, save your poor little cousins . . . think of how easy it would be to let a rich man take care of you. . . .*

It was the same deceitful voice that had haunted me in the bathroom when the killers were near—the one that had told me to cry out and bring death down upon us to end the torment. I knew then, as I knew now, that it was the devil's voice. I understood that whenever God's light is dimmed by despair, the devil finds a perch from which to whisper in our ears. The enemy never sleeps; he waits for our moments of weakness to strike at us with temptation.

I knelt down on the road right then and there and asked God to keep that dark voice away from me.

Then I thought about Jesus and how he'd encouraged the disciples to keep fishing even though their nets remained empty. When they put their trust in Jesus, they wound up with more fish than their nets could hold. That was the kind of faith I needed in order to find my place at the UN. *Dear Jesus,* I prayed, *keep my heart pure and my faith strong. Give me the strength to find work where none exists. Get my job application onto the desk of someone important, someone who can hire me. Please find a way for them to see past my rags. I trust in you, and I trust that you will take care of me. Amen.*

I got up off my knees and made a mental list of what I needed to get a job. It was a short one, consisting solely of new clothes and my school records. But how would I get them? I had no money to shop, and my records were 200 miles away at my old university, a trip I'd never be able to make on my own.

Just then, a car stopped beside me and honked its horn. I looked up to see a former professor of mine from the university, who was driving back to campus the very next day and agreed to give me a ride.

MY DORM ROOM HAD BEEN LOOTED, but I found my school transcripts. I also unearthed $30 I'd hidden away before the genocide, which was a fortune to me now. I took a taxi back to Kigali, bought new clothes, and had my hair done. Within two days of asking Jesus for help to get a job, I was in a new suit and at the front gate of the UN. This time the security guard waved me through with a smile, and I held my transcripts confidently in my hand as I marched to the personnel director's office. I felt poised, pretty, self-assured, and ready to take on the world.

Unfortunately, my enthusiasm was crushed when the director's secretary rejected my application after barely looking at it. In a pinched and condescending voice, she told me that there was no work for me at the UN and probably never would be. "Close the door on your way out," she said, and turned her back to me.

I was so devastated I quickly left the office in tears and exited by the back stairs. But as I made my way down the steps, I ran into the one man at the United Nations who could truly help me. Pierre Mehu was the chief spokesperson for the UN's mission in Rwanda, and an angel sent to me from heaven. He told me to visit his office the next day, where he asked me about my experiences during the genocide. I told him everything about my family and what had happened to me in the pastor's bathroom. He was so moved by my story that he decided to take me under his wing.

"I'm going to get you a job here," he promised, "but I want you to know that I'll never expect anything from you except for you to be true to yourself and your beliefs. I can only imagine how proud your parents must have been of you and how much they loved you. I want you to look at me as a father, and let the UN be like a home to you. If you have any problems, Immaculée, you come straight to me, and I'll take care of everything. Please think of me as someone you can trust."

My spirits soared. I wanted to jump up and down in the hallway and scream, "Praise God!" But I didn't want to look too unprofessional before I was officially hired, so I just said, "Thank you, sir," and shook his hand.

Mr. Mehu kept his word and took very good care of me. He arranged for a week of intense typing and English lessons so that I'd be well prepared for the UN's mandatory proficiency exam—which, thanks to his kindness, I passed with flying colors.

Within two weeks, I'd been hired into the UN's secretarial pool and was training for my first job as a filing clerk. It wasn't a glamorous position, but it certainly was miraculous. My salary was $300 a month; I was making more money than any Rwandan I'd ever known. My first check was enough for me to get my aunts and cousins out of the refugee camp and set them up in a house near Mataba, where, despite what had happened, they felt most at home. I had enough money left over to send some to my brother Aimable and buy 200 crayons—just enough to bring a little color into the life of every orphan at Mother Teresa's.

God had made me rich in so many ways, and I was overjoyed to share the wealth!

CHAPTER 10

OFFICE POLITICS

Six months after he found me a job at the United Nations, tragedy touched the life of my adopted father, Pierre Mehu.

True to his promise at our first meeting, Mr. Mehu had been a constant source of encouragement and support for me at work. He was never gloomy or cross with anyone on his staff, and his cheery daily greeting to me ("Good morning, daughter!") always put a smile on my face. So when I came into the office early one morning and found him quietly weeping at his desk, I knew that something terrible had happened.

"Mr. Mehu, is there anything I can get you, sir?" I asked tentatively. I was unsure if I should intrude on his privacy, but my heart ached to see him suffer alone.

"Oh, Immaculée, now I can understand a bit of your grief. My son Benoit was mugged in New York City last night . . . they shot him, and I don't even know how many times he was wounded. He's in a coma, and no one can tell me if he's going to live or die. He needs his father, but I'm so far away. Why did I let him go there to study—why didn't I keep him closer to home where he'd be safe?"

"I will pray for God to watch over Benoit and bring him back to you, sir," I said, putting my hand on his shoulder. Mr. Mehu looked up and gave me a weak smile, as his tears splashed onto my arm.

A little later, Mr. Mehu brought a very tall man to my office. The stranger was dressed in traditional African clothing, although I didn't know which country or tribe he was from: He was wearing a flowing, gold-colored tunic that was heavily embroidered with intricate needlepoint designs; along with a dark red fez-style hat, which added another six inches to his already-imposing height. The man had to duck to clear the doorway, and he looked down at me like a storybook giant.

"I'd like you to meet Khadim Modou Adama, my dearest friend at the UN," Mr. Mehu told me. "He'll be taking over for me."

I offered my hand to the tall man, and it disappeared into his enormous palm. "It's nice to meet you, Mr. Adama, but . . . ," I trailed off. Turning to Mr. Mehu in confusion, I asked, "What do you mean 'taking over for' you, sir?"

"I put in for early retirement," he replied. "I'm leaving for New York at the end of the week to be with Benoit."

Oh, not again! Everyone I get close to is taken away, I thought, and immediately chastised myself for being so selfish. Of course Mr. Mehu had to leave—he needed to be with his son, and his son needed his father.

"Don't look so upset, daughter. Khadim is going to take over my work duties temporarily, but he'll be taking on my 'Immaculée duty' full-time. He's going to fill in for me as your second father, your UN dad." He turned to his friend and said, "You mustn't let anything happen to this young lady when I'm gone. Don't let any of the men around here take advantage of her. God made this child my responsibility, and now she is yours, all right?"

"Of course, Pierre," Mr. Adama agreed with a smile. His voice wasn't at all what I expected from this huge man: It was gentle, playful, and imbued with such genuine tenderness that I was instantly at ease with him. "I have three daughters who are about the same age as this girl, and I'll protect her as if she were my

98

own." To me, he promised, "Don't you worry about anything. I'm going to take good care of you."

I wasn't sure why Mr. Mehu and Mr. Adama felt I needed taking care of; no one had bothered me at the UN, and my six months there had been wonderful. Even though I was now living with Sarah and her family, I'd met some military officers who'd kindly escorted me back to Mataba several times—even once by helicopter! My paychecks were delivered on schedule, I was given jobs with greater responsibility, and my supervisors seemed pleased with my work.

But within a month of Mr. Mehu's departure, I understood how much he'd been shielding me from unpleasantness and harm, as well as how much I'd rely on Khadim Modou Adama for the same paternal protection.

As soon as Mr. Mehu left, Mr. Adama stepped into his role as my adopted father, and he really was like yet another dad. I thanked God for bringing him to me as much as I'd thanked Him for Mr. Mehu. Speaking of God, Mr. Adama loved talking to me about Him and the importance of praying. He was a devout Muslim and never missed any of the five daily calls to prayer required by his faith. Even if we were in a group discussion about work, when the little chime on his wristwatch rang, he'd say, "Please excuse me for a few minutes." Then he'd go into his office, roll his mat out on the floor, kneel in the direction of Mecca, and begin to pray.

I loved how he never worried about closing his office door during prayers; like me, he loved talking to God and was never embarrassed if others overheard the conversation. He used to say that when it came to prayer, we had an open-door policy with God.

Mr. Adama's wife and daughters lived in France, where he'd been a high-ranking official in the diplomatic service, and he visited them frequently. He usually returned from his trips with clothes for me from Paris, which were accompanied by letters from each of his three girls. They told me about their life in France, what their schools were like, and how their dad never tired of talking about me and the way I'd survived the genocide by praying. The letters always made me feel as if I had sisters living in a peaceful, glamorous place that I might visit one day.

Every morning when Mr. Adama came into the office, he'd say, "Immaculée, you are too skinny; Mr. Mehu will be angry with me. Go get something to eat—that's an order!" Then he'd give some money to Kingston, one of the supervisors in my office, and tell him to take me for breakfast. It wasn't hard to see that Kingston didn't like being told what to do, but Mr. Adama had a much more senior rank than he did.

Kingston would take the money and escort me to the cafeteria, where he'd buy himself a huge morning meal of meat and eggs, while I'd sip on a cup of tea and nibble on a piece of cheese. Between mouthfuls of sausage, he'd say, "It's a good thing Adama likes you so much, Immaculée. I get lots of free protein every day."

Kingston was a good-natured, laid-back fellow from the Caribbean, but he was also very vain. He was a bodybuilder with a habit of strutting through the office, curling his arms, and asking the secretaries to feel his big biceps. Sometimes he'd stand in front of a mirror for long stretches of time and admire himself as he flexed his muscles. And whenever a new girl was assigned to our office, Kingston would tell her to bring her workout clothes to the UN gym to join the office aerobics class. He'd then give the girl—who had yet to learn to avoid him—a personal-training session, putting his hands on her arms and legs to adjust her body into the stances needed for the exercise.

Although he'd asked me to go many times, I never joined his "class." I hadn't heard the word *aerobics* before I worked at the UN, and the idea of people jumping around in a room to get thin seemed silly to me. Rwandans seldom got fat because they never had extra food to eat, and they got plenty of exercise by walking everywhere they went, whether it was down the hill to get water or several miles to get to school. Anyway, Kingston was conceited and fancied himself a ladies' man, but he was friendly to me and seemed harmless. However, not everybody was friendly to me, and a few were not harmless at all.

Office Politics

My first taste of office politics came when I began having lunch with a co-worker named Annick, a young Tutsi woman from Tanzania who was the same age I was. At first we hit it off: I told her what it was like to grow up in Rwanda, and she shared childhood stories about being raised in a country where there were more Muslim mosques than churches and where you could drive to the Indian Ocean for holidays.

But our friendship soured when Annick started having an affair with Robert, a military officer attached to the UN. Robert's steady girlfriend, DeeDee, worked in our office . . . and was Annick's best friend. Once the affair started, Annick couldn't think of anything to talk about except how wonderful Robert was or how stupid DeeDee was for not seeing what was happening right under her nose.

"Honestly, Immaculée, I can sit with DeeDee for hours and get her to tell me all the things she does to please Robert and make him happy, and then I use all her tricks when I get him alone. Sometimes the three of us go out together, and she's so clueless that I can practically sit on his lap! I'll be able to steal her boyfriend from her, and she won't know it happened until I invite her to our wedding," Annick gloated. "DeeDee and her entire family are Hutus, so she deserves any misery a Tutsi can send her way—it serves her right."

She spoke with such contempt and cruelty about DeeDee that I couldn't fathom why she'd pretend to be her friend. "But DeeDee thinks you and she are so close," I protested. "She trusts you. And it doesn't matter if she's a Hutu; she's still a person. What you're doing isn't fair or right."

"Oh, come on, Immaculée. Why should you care about the feelings of a Hutu after what happened to your family? Besides, Robert is a good catch, and nowadays you have to look out for number one. Don't be so naïve."

It turned out that quite a few women in the office knew about the affair, and I'd hear them snicker whenever DeeDee walked by. The poor woman had no idea what was being said about her, and it felt terrible to see her being so cruelly deceived. I didn't understand how people could be so mean and nasty. Hadn't we learned anything from the cruelty that had devastated our country?

Even though I didn't know DeeDee personally, I decided that I couldn't stand by and let her be treated in such a wicked and degrading manner. I shyly approached her one afternoon and asked if I could buy her a cup of tea after work. She was suspicious at first, as Rwandans didn't tend to ask complete strangers to go out with them—especially since I was Tutsi and she was Hutu. It was also odd in our culture for a woman to ask another woman she didn't know to go somewhere. But DeeDee agreed to join me, and we met at a restaurant near the UN.

"You must think I'm crazy for asking you out like this," I told her, embarrassed that I was about to tell a woman I'd only just met that her boyfriend was cheating on her with her closest friend.

"Well, I thought it was a little strange . . . but people around the office say you pray all the time, so I figured you probably weren't dangerous. I started praying a lot myself after all the killing started. I heard you're Tutsi, and I want you to know that my family didn't hurt anyone. My brother was killed for not joining the Interahamwe, and soldiers stole all of my dad's beer and liquor before they pistol-whipped him and burned down his tavern. We had nothing left after the war except each other. Most of my friends were Tutsis, and they're all dead now."

DeeDee's honesty and openness made me like her right away. Although we'd go on to become very good friends in the months to come, our relationship got off to a bumpy start when I blurted out, "You have to break it off with Robert; he's no good. He's having an affair with Annick, and she's no good either. She's a false friend who wants to hurt you. It's not like me to tell people such terrible things, but you seem so nice that I couldn't let you go on being deceived by their lies."

DeeDee was stunned by what I said and refused to believe me at first, but I kept telling her over and over that it was the truth. Finally, she put two and two together and didn't like what it added up to. She decided to confront Robert about the affair, which he denied. However, DeeDee started keeping a close eye on his behavior, especially when Annick was around, and she discovered the truth on her own. She broke up with Robert, ended her friendship with Annick, and was happy to be rid of both of them.

AFTER DEEDEE ENDED THINGS WITH ROBERT, I felt as though I'd spoiled the fun for some of the women at the office . . . who now turned their attention on me. I assumed that Annick had told them I wasn't to be trusted, or maybe they'd been gossiping about me all along and I hadn't noticed. But sure enough, my reputation started to be called into question.

I suppose it started after I had, despite my meager diet, regained the weight I'd lost during the genocide. When I went into hiding, I weighed 115 pounds; when I emerged, I weighed 65 pounds. I looked like a skeleton: My eyes had retreated deeply into my skull, loose skin hung from my arms and legs where there once had been only solid muscle, and it was easy to see where the curve of my rib cage met my spine. But as the months went by, I filled out and started looking like my young, healthy self again. In addition, for the first time in my life, I had a bit of money to spend on my appearance—I could afford to have my hair done, buy a little makeup, and splurge on some pretty outfits.

My mother had always made my clothes and insisted I wear modest dresses that often came down to my ankles. We had a strict dress code at my Catholic high school, and I had very little money to spend on a wardrobe at university, so I tended to wear whatever my mother made for me. Now I had a paycheck, and after buying groceries, sending cash to my aunts and brother, and getting books and toys for the orphans, I could give myself a little allowance.

I felt like a bird that had been let out of a cage. I bought some pretty blouses and skirts that were far shorter than anything I'd ever worn—some even hung several inches above my knees. My clothes were fashionable and made me feel good about myself, and there was nothing sinful about my attire. My poor mother, however, would have been horrified!

Like a teenager who could express herself for the first time in a bright and happy way, I felt free of the confines of a drab and uncomfortable wardrobe. I kept telling myself that life was short, and the world was too gray and dreary already. Why shouldn't I liven it up a bit? Why not find some enjoyment in simple, every-day things? Besides, what was wrong with dressing up? I knew that God wanted me to feel happy . . . unfortunately, many of my co-workers did not.

When I walked past in a new skirt, I could hear many of the women whispering to each other, and when I had to drop off a report or some paperwork to one of the supervisors' secretaries, I often received a nasty look that made me feel dirty. DeeDee told me that Annick had started a gossip campaign about me, suggesting that I was getting new clothes from the guys I was dating. Nothing could have been further from the truth, but I couldn't deny that men at the UN began acting strangely around me soon after Mr. Mehu left.

Suddenly, lots of my male co-workers started to ogle me. It didn't matter if they were single or married—they approached me and asked me to go dancing with them, or out on dates, or away somewhere for a weekend, or even to marry them! Some were so vulgar as to offer me money to spend time with them. I refused every single proposition; not only was I still in mourning with no interest in romance, but I had a strict curfew at Sarah's house and never broke it.

For a while I felt flattered that the opposite sex found me attractive. When I'd come out of hiding, I'd felt absolutely hideous and was certain no man would ever look at me again, so the attention was a compliment. But the more the men doted on me, the more I was gossiped about by the women. It was a very hurtful time. I didn't understand what I was doing wrong: I couldn't help the way men acted around me, and I definitely wasn't trying to provoke them. I grew up in a family where sex was never, ever mentioned; and we certainly didn't have any sex-education classes in Catholic school. My parents and the nuns made sure that I knew what kind of behavior would offend God.

Before the genocide, Rwandan men had always treated me with respect and dignity, so I was unprepared for the freewheeling attitude of the foreign men at the UN. Nor was I ready to be judged so harshly for how I looked. I started to understand why my mother had been so protective and disapproving of outer beauty. She hadn't let people call me pretty when I was little because she wanted me to grow up focused on inner beauty, and I hoped she knew that I was still a good girl. God certainly knew that my heart and body were clean and pure.

I told myself not to worry about how others viewed me; all that mattered was how I appeared in His eyes. And He had sent me many gentlemen who always acted honorably around me and treated me with respect, such as Mr. Mehu and Mr. Adama. These men gave me friendship that I could value and rely upon throughout my life.

CHAPTER 11

OFFICE PREDATORS

The unwanted advances from men at my workplace escalated from upsetting annoyances to sexual harassment and physical intimidation. It began when one of the biggest bosses at the United Nations sent word for me to come to his office. I had no idea why I'd been summoned and was worried it was because of the gossip swirling around me.

When I arrived, his secretary gave me a hard look and said, "Sit here and wait. The chief will call you when he's ready." Her icy greeting didn't put me at ease; I could feel the perspiration running down my back. It seemed like an eternity before the office door opened and "the chief" beckoned me into his room with a wave of his fingers—one of which was encircled by a thick gold wedding band.

He was a good-looking man with such dark, glowing skin that I thought he must polish his face in the morning. His office was the most spacious I'd seen at the UN and decorated with wooden masks, shields, and other native-African creations. On his large desk sat framed pictures of his wife and children, along with several of himself. I was so nervous that I decided to stand in the center of the room with my head down, my eyes fixed upon the lion-skin rug my toes were touching.

"I've heard your story, Immaculée."

I glanced up and saw that he had placed himself in front of a full-length mirror with his back toward me, and he was admiring the expensive-looking black suit he was wearing. As he adjusted his tie, he turned his head slightly, and our eyes met in the looking glass.

"Your parents are dead? You have one surviving brother in Senegal? Isn't that right?"

"That's correct, sir."

"Don't call me 'sir.' Call me 'E.'"

"Yes, Mr. E."

"Not 'mister,' just 'E.' That is my Christian name."

"Yes, sir."

"How often do you see your brother in Senegal . . . what's his name?"

"His name is Aimable, and I haven't seen him since the genocide. We can't afford to visit yet, sir."

"Call me 'E.'"

"Yes, Mr. E."

"So, Immaculée, your parents are dead, and your brother is on the other side of Africa. That basically makes you an orphan, doesn't it?"

"No, Mr. E, I live with a good family and have aunts in Kibuye."

"Yes, yes, I know about your aunts and that you live with friends," he replied impatiently. "But you're basically an orphan, right?"

Why does he keep asking if I'm an orphan? And why does he keep his back to me? Why am I here? I wondered, at a complete loss. To him, I said, "Yes sir, I am. But I have people that I—"

"I understand that," he broke in. "But what I wanted to say to you is that, seeing as you're basically an orphan, I would like to buy you a house."

"Pardon me?"

"A house, Immaculée, your own house. I think you'd be more comfortable. And perhaps you'd like to return to school. Is it true that you didn't complete university?"

"Why would you buy me a house, sir? I don't understand."

"I told you to call me 'E.' I will buy you a house because I want to take care of you; I want to take care of everything for you. And you can take care of me. You're an orphan, after all—you have no one else."

My heart began to pound. What did he mean by "take care of everything"? What did *everything* mean? And what did he mean that *I* could take care of *him?* My palms were slick from sweat. I was afraid of this man, who easily could have me fired or put on the street or in a refugee camp.

That's when I heard the sickly sweet voice again, the evil force urging me not to think, but to yield . . . not to question what was being asked of me but just to grab what was being offered: *Say yes, Immaculée. Take the freedom; take the money. Fly Aimable home every weekend, set your aunts up for life, go to school—you love school—get your Ph.D. Think of it—Dr. Ilibagiza! Why not? You can relax and let someone take care of you for a change . . . just say yes.*

"Cat got your tongue, Immaculée?" Mr. E demanded. When I didn't respond, he grinned and said, "So, I take it the answer is yes?"

"What? I mean, pardon me?"

My face was burning; there was no air in the room. Mr. E had turned from the mirror and was now standing right in front of me. He was so close to me that I stepped back and rubbed my eyes, trying to clear my mind.

I felt a calming presence, like an angel by my side, which gently asked me, *What are you thinking? This man wants you to be his mistress—"taking care" of him means <u>sleeping with</u> him, Immaculée, selling your body for all those gifts. Nothing is for free with this man, who can destroy you. There is evil here, so walk away. But do be careful.*

I cleared my throat and told Mr. E, "I thank you for the generous offer, sir, but I'd like to think it over. I'll get back to you soon."

"What is there to think over? You're alone with no one to take care of you . . . I will."

"God takes care of me, sir."

"God?" Mr. E said with a laugh. "God can't buy you food or nice clothes or pay for your tuition, but I can. And don't think that your *daddies,* Mehu or Adama, will look out for you either. Mehu is long gone, and Adama isn't going to be around much longer. I thought you were a smart girl; you have to think of your future. You're young, so enjoy yourself now and worry about God later. I'll buy you a house near a church, if that makes you happy."

"Thank you just the same, sir, but I really have to think it over. I'll call you at the end of the week," I replied quickly and backed out of the room. "Thank you again, sir."

Mr. E's secretary glared at me as I opened the door and hurried into the hall.

My hands were still shaking when I got back to my desk. I wanted to go find DeeDee, but I knew that I wouldn't be able to tell anyone about what had happened in Mr. E's office. Who would believe me? Mr. E was a powerful man: He advised the president on political policy; he had bodyguards, a chauffeur, and his own limousine; and people bowed down to him. Who was I? I was nothing—a miserable holocaust survivor trying to get money from the great man. That's what people would say. They would shame me, and say that I tried to seduce him. I couldn't even go to Mr. Adama for advice because he'd only bring trouble upon himself by defending me.

What kind of men work for the United Nations? My mind raced. *They're married! Do they forget about their wives and families as soon as they leave their own countries? The UN is supposed to help people in trouble, not take advantage of them!* But I couldn't make such broad generalizations; lumping people into groups had led to the genocide and all the suffering afterward. I couldn't blame the UN for Mr. E, and I couldn't blame Mr. E for the others who were harassing me. All I could do was pray.

Dear Father, Your daughter is in trouble. I am beset by wickedness. Please guide my choices, lead me through all my days and nights, keep

my heart clean in the presence of loveless men, and make me strong.
Thank You, my Dear One. Amen.

AFTER THINKING LONG AND HARD ABOUT WHAT TO DO, I decided to do nothing. I had no intention of getting back to Mr. E, so I planned to do everything I could to avoid him. But after my uncomfortable meeting with him, he started walking by my desk in the mornings to say hello, although I'd never seen him in my office before. Every time he walked into the room, the other women cast judgmental stares at me, and I could hear them whispering. Mr. E would linger in the office and chat with Kingston, staring at me all the while. I'd just keep my head down and shuffle papers until he left.

"You seem good at making friends in high places, Immaculée," Kingston remarked after one of Mr. E's morning appearances. "Here's a little tip, though: don't get on E's bad side. If he likes you, you can do very well by him. If he doesn't like you . . . well, just make sure he likes you. That's what I do, I make sure I get him whatever he asks for, on time and with a smile."

Kingston's job was to order and distribute imported goods to the UN staff and district offices, but he also took private requests from top-ranking officials and knew all their special wants and desires. And I could see that he knew Mr. E quite well.

I didn't like what Kingston might be implying, but I had to assume that he was only trying to give me good advice. He'd always been nice to me, and although he embarrassed me when he stood in front of me and flexed his muscles, we got along very well. He'd even done me a huge favor the week before by arranging a job for my friend Sarah at another UN office.

Kingston smiled at me now and said, "You have to be a people pleaser; that's the secret to getting ahead. Look at me: three promotions in one year."

Despite Kingston's suggestion, after a week of Mr. E's daily visits, I decided that I had no choice but to go to Mr. Adama with my problem or it would get worse. But I was stopped dead in my tracks before reaching his office—through his open door, I saw him having a very friendly conversation with Mr. E. They were both laughing and smiling, and then Mr. E reached out and patted Mr. Adama's shoulder.

Oh no, what kind of relationship do these two have? I worried. *Are they good friends? Does Mr. Adama know what Mr. E has been asking of me?*

Mr. Adama had promised to be my adopted father, but how could I ask him for a father's protection when he was friends with the man I needed protection from?

How I missed my real dad! If he were here, he would be beside himself. He would drag Mr. E into the street and thrash him for his shameful disrespect.

When I left work that night, I was too exhausted to walk to Sarah's, so I climbed into one of the minibuses the UN used to shuttle employees to and from their homes. The stress of being stalked by Mr. E was draining my energy. At university, I'd heard about sexual harassment in other countries, but I'd never thought about what it meant until it happened to me. How many young women suffered the same type of torment because an unethical man had power over their livelihood? I felt as helpless as I had when the killers were hunting me.

As three or four other women got into the bus and it pulled up to the security gate, I silently asked God, *Why am I back in this kind of situation? Maybe You want me to help someone else facing similar circumstances. . . . You must want me to learn a lesson from this, and I accept that, but does it have to be such a long lesson? Can't You wrap it up, Lord?*

Just then, the windshield of the minibus shattered, and a metallic pinging echoed through the little vehicle. While the driver was rapidly backing the bus away from the UN's main entrance, I could see a group of about 50 men—most of them were quite young, but others were middle-aged or even elderly—tossing pieces of broken brick at the security gate from across the street. They were yelling at the guards who had been posted along the fence, "Get out of Rwanda! UN, go home! Run away and desert us like you did during the genocide! UN, go home. Leave our women alone! UN, get out; run away home!"

"Sorry, too many demonstrators to drive today," the driver told us, sliding the side door open. "It's safer for you to use the back exit and walk home."

With each passing month, more and more protesters had gathered outside UN headquarters, and the demonstrations had become increasingly violent. Many Rwandans hated the United Nations for pulling almost all of its troops out of Rwanda after the genocide started. Only a handful of peacekeepers had remained under the command of the Canadian general Roméo Dallaire, a brave man who refused orders to abandon Kigali. Everybody believed that if the UN had kept its forces in Rwanda, the genocide would have been much smaller, or would never have happened at all. A lot of my compatriots considered Rwandans who worked at the UN to be traitors, and it was worse if you were a woman.

Rwandan men were very protective of their women and believed that UN foreigners were corrupting them, making them mistresses and then leaving them alone and pregnant when their tours of duty were finished. The men behind the gates shouted that UN workers were turning good girls into sex slaves. While it was easy to understand why the protesters felt the way they did, I hated the violence and anger, and I thought that the demonstrations overlooked the good work the UN was doing in our country.

I slipped out the back way, and instead of going straight home, I hiked to Mother Teresa's to visit the orphans. I knew that I'd be reenergized by their undemanding and unqualified love. Earlier in the week I'd found an illustrated children's Bible and couldn't wait to share the pictures and stories with the boys and girls. It struck me as funny that, even in African Bibles that were written in Kinyarwanda, Jesus was always portrayed as a white man with beautiful blue eyes and long, blonde hair. I used to laugh when a group of European volunteers would come to the orphanage, and the children would point to them in awe and say, "Look how many Jesuses have come to see us."

My favorite picture in the Bible I was taking to the orphanage was of Jesus gathering the little boys and girls to him as he sat in a pasture, tending sheep. The caption was from Luke: "Suffer little children to come unto me, and forbid them not, for of such is the kingdom of God."

THE FOLLOWING MONDAY, I WAS AGAIN SUMMONED to Mr. E's office and was certain that he was going to fire me. This time his secretary didn't even look at me; she just pointed to the open door and sent me directly into the chief's big office.

Mr. E was standing on his lion-skin rug with a disappointed look on his face, his hands clasped. He immediately said, "You were going to call me by the end of the week, isn't that right? But you didn't. Why not?"

"I saw you in the office during the week, sir, and you always looked so busy that I didn't want to disturb you."

"I see. Well, do you accept my offer?"

Please, God, don't let me lose my job for speaking the truth, I quickly prayed. I told Mr. E, "No, sir, I do not accept. I'll stay where I am. It's a good Christian home with a good Christian family, and I try to live my life as Christ instructed."

Mr. E stared at me blankly, uncertain how to respond. "Well, I'm busy right now, Immaculée," he finally managed, "but I have reservations at a very expensive restaurant this evening. I would enjoy it very much if you joined me for dinner, and we can settle this matter in an agreeable way."

"I'm sorry, sir. I have a strict curfew and must go home immediately from my visit to the orphanage after work. But we could have lunch in the cafeteria tomorrow if you like."

"Don't be ridiculous—we can't have lunch! I can't be seen with you here; I have a reputation to maintain."

I was so insulted and angry that I wanted to slap his face. He was the one acting despicably, yet *he* would be ashamed to be seen with *me!* I kept my hands at my side and replied, "I'm sorry that things turned out this way. Good day to you, sir."

I walked out of his office expecting to see a pink slip waiting for me when I got back to my desk. But I heard nothing from Mr. E for the rest of the week. I hoped that after our last meeting he would understand that I lived according to God's rules, not Mr. E's.

That Friday, Kingston asked me to have lunch with him, as he often did at the end of the week. He'd booked a car from the motor pool, saying that he was taking me somewhere nice to eat.

"Where are we going?" I asked when I got in the car—happy that a supervisor was being so nice to me, but a bit nervous because of Kingston's association with Mr. E.

"We're going to the Hotel Umubano."

"The Umubano! That's a little too expensive for my tastes, Kingston."

"Don't worry about the money."

"But I always worry about how things are paid for."

"It's my treat. Don't worry about a thing, Immaculée. Go with the flow," he said in his singsong Caribbean accent.

The Umubano was half a mile away from central Kigali and located at the top of a hill. My eyes danced over the tennis courts, terraces, botanical gardens, and huge outdoor swimming pool as we drove up the hill and into the driveway. It was the nicest hotel I'd ever seen; but then again, since I'd grown up in a poor village, I was easily impressed.

A uniformed bellhop opened the car door and led us inside. At the restaurant, the maître d' greeted Kingston by name and escorted us to the rear of the dining area, where a private table shielded by a wooden trestle had been prepared for us. And sitting at that table, drinking a glass of whiskey, was Mr. E.

I looked back at Kingston in anger. I was so hurt by his betrayal, yet he just shrugged his shoulders.

Mr. E stood up, pulled out a chair for me to sit beside him, and said, "Ah, Immaculée, I'm so glad you accepted my invitation. The food is magnificent here. Would you like a drink?"

"I'll just have water, please."

"Are you sure?"

"Yes, sir."

"I told you, call me 'E.'"

"Yes, *sir*."

I was so mad at myself for getting into such an awkward situation, but I was afraid, too. Mr. E and Kingston had tricked me into lunch—what were they planning for dessert? I decided not to show them that I was upset or nervous. I'd play it cool and watch for a chance to escape.

The lunch passed quickly and with little conversation. I had no appetite, so Kingston ate the steak ordered for me. After finishing his third whiskey, Mr. E banged his glass on the table and announced that lunch was finished: "I have to pick up some government-policy papers in my suite. Follow me, please."

Mr. E's tone made it plain that he wasn't making a request. Kingston walked behind me, his hulking body filling the hallway and making it impossible for me to turn around and walk away. I reached into my purse and clasped my father's red and white rosary tightly in my hand. Those precious beads had comforted me during the most harrowing and dangerous hours of my life, and I was counting on them now.

We rode the elevator to the top floor and entered a small sitting room in Mr. E's suite. "Make yourselves comfortable," he said, disappearing into the bedroom. Kingston picked up a chair from a writing desk, put it in front of the door, and sat down. I looked at him and let my eyes speak for me: *How dare you?!* Again, he shrugged his shoulders.

My anger dissolved as my situation snapped into focus. Kingston and Mr. E had clearly worked out a plan, but a plan to do what? They had duped me into coming to a hotel on the outskirts of town and bullied me into a private room—the only way out was blocked by a muscle-bound goon. My mouth was dry, and I started trembling. I hated that I was frightened of these men, but I was. I felt so foolish, weak, and helpless.

Kingston leaned back until the top of his chair was pressing against the door and folded his bulging arms across his chest. He stared at the wall in front of him with the same lifeless look I'd witnessed in the eyes of the killers during the genocide. How many times had I seen good people embrace evil this way?

Oh no, they're going to rape me! I realized. I held on to my rosary, and my heart and mind cried out with all their might: *Please send*

Your angels to help me, God! I swear that I'll help other women avoid these situations, but don't let them touch me, Lord, <u>please!</u>

"Come in here for a minute, Immaculée," Mr. E ordered from the other room. Kingston kept staring at the wall as I moved into the bedroom, and Mr. E stepped around me to close the door. He'd taken off his tie, and his jacket was draped over an armchair. "Sit down," he said, pointing to the bed.

I looked at the bed, at Mr. E, and then through the glass doors that led to the balcony. The pool was below us, surrounded by a cobblestone walk.

All I have to do is jump. . . .

I could see Kigali tucked into the green hills, set against the mist-shrouded mountain range far in the distance. From here, the city's suffering was hidden—Rwanda's capital looked serene and pretty from so high above. God's beauty was even in this sordid room, if only these men would open their hearts.

What beauty You have created, Lord, I silently told Him. You truly can do anything . . . please make these men look beyond themselves, beyond their own lust and contempt. Make them see the beauty in all You have created. And if they refuse to see, then give me the strength to fight them in Your name. I am Your daughter. I know You will protect me!

"Isn't my country beautiful?" I asked Mr. E. I was still staring at the mountains, refusing to acknowledge his invitation to bed. I hoped that he'd be stirred by the majesty of God, not the beast within him. "There is a very old saying in my country, which states that after God spends all day visiting every other place on Earth, He comes home to Rwanda to sleep. That's because, of all the lands He created, Rwanda is the most beautiful. Can't you see that, sir? Can't you see God everywhere?"

"I'm not interested in God or Rwanda, Immaculée, I'm interested in you. I could take you now if I wanted, but I'm trying to be a nice guy. I can be generous, very generous. I am a good-looking man, and I am very rich. I will make you rich, too; all you have to do is say yes. Now decide!"

What an insulting brute! I thought. What kind of man is this—so important and powerful, yet so stupid and blind! He brags about being rich at the same time he begs me to feed his ego!

I was no longer afraid of Mr. E, and I was no longer afraid of Kingston. I felt sorry for these men, who only looked for material gain or physical gratification, never caring whom they hurt to satisfy their wants. Looking at Mr. E, I now saw him for what he was: a weak and pleading man with a dirty mind standing by the edge of a hotel bed. All he saw when he looked at me was an orphan he could mistreat without fear of getting caught or facing the consequences. It was all too familiar, and God had helped me through far worse situations with men far more vicious and depraved than Mr. E.

What good did he think his power would do him when he faced God? How could he think his money would protect him when all he had could be snatched away from him in an instant?

I wanted to tell him about meeting Mupundu, who'd been a big politician in the Hutu government and the richest woman in Mataba . . . until she gave in to the bloodlust of the genocide. I saw her limping back to our village from Zaire, and she'd lost everything—her money, her power, her family. She didn't even have shoes to cover her bleeding feet. She'd turned from God, and she'd lost the only real thing she could count on, just as surely as Mr. E would lose everything unless he turned his heart away from wickedness and back to the Lord.

"I told you to decide, Immaculée," he demanded now. "Or would you like me to make the decision for you?"

"Look out that window, *sir!*" I shouted at Mr. E. "Do you see my country? Do you see Rwanda? Do you have any idea what we have been through here? Do you have any idea what *I* have been through? I wasn't born an orphan, Mr. E! My family was butchered—I was turned into an orphan by people who set the devil free in their hearts. You know the kind of people I mean, sir. You may scare me to death by bringing me to this room; you may even hurt me or have me fired and thrown on the street. But you can't take away the values my family gave me, and you can't take away what God has given me. I'm already rich, sir, and I don't have to decide anything. The answer has always been *no!*"

Mr. E was furious, but he didn't come near me. He picked up his jacket, opened the door, and barked at Kingston, "Get up, let's go! I'm late!" Before they walked out of the room, Mr. E turned to me and flatly said, "I didn't come here to be rejected by a little beggar refugee. You don't have to tell me where you came from; I know exactly where you came from . . . and I think you'll find it hard to be so high and mighty when I send you back there." He slammed the door, leaving me alone in his room.

Thank You for giving me Your strength to face them, Lord . . . but does this mean I'm fired?

By the time I got back to the office, a new nightmare had begun.

AFTER THE HOTEL INCIDENT, Kingston wouldn't make eye contact with me, but he showed up at my desk every hour with a new stack of forms that I hadn't been trained to fill out. It happened again the next day, and the next. I was staying at work later and later but still couldn't catch up.

For the first time, I was called into my boss's office to account for the delays and mistakes I was making. I was asked many embarrassing questions I couldn't answer: Why had my work fallen off so suddenly? Was I getting enough sleep, perhaps staying up too late at night? Was I having emotional problems? Was my filing job too complicated? Would it be better if they found someone to replace me and let me look for work elsewhere?

Mr. E was making good on his threat. He was putting me on the street, but he was taking his time and enjoying it—pushing me out the door with a thousand pieces of paper and a hundred belittling remarks. It seemed that my career at the United Nations was coming to a humiliating end, along with the security it had given me. When I received a message that Mr. Adama wanted to see me, I assumed that in a final twist of vengeance, Mr. E had assigned the task of firing me to the man I most admired at the UN.

But when I entered Mr. Adama's office, he jumped to his feet, closed the door, and began apologizing for every hurtful thing Mr. E had done. "I'm so sorry this happened to you, my child. I should have stopped it long ago," he insisted. "When I heard that E was paying so much attention to you, I wanted to ask you if he was up to no good. But I didn't want to embarrass you by making assumptions or intruding on your privacy. I thought that if you needed my help you'd come to me, and if you didn't, I should mind my own business."

"I didn't want to cause you trouble, Mr. Adama."

"Cause *me* trouble? You have no idea what kind of trouble I can cause when I want to—I've been in this game a long time, and I've dealt with the likes of E before. I don't know how these men reach such high positions, but I'm afraid it happens too often. Yet as big as he is, you stung him. I don't know what you said to him, but you stung him good . . . and then he tried to sting me."

"Did he do something to hurt you, sir?"

"No, Immaculée, he's not big enough to hurt me. He's bold enough to try, though. He came into my office and threatened me, saying that if I didn't stop helping you and treating you like a daughter, people would begin to hear rumors that I was sleeping with you. The nerve of the man! I yelled at him, telling him the reason I treat you like a daughter is because you *are* a daughter to me—and he'd better think twice before he said anything else about you or hurt you in any way."

Mr. Adama was shouting now, calling on Allah to curse Mr. E. He moved frantically around the room, dragging his long African dress behind him. "I almost hit him, Immaculée!" he continued, raising his massive hand above his head and shaking it in the air. "I stood over him with my arm up here, and I swear I almost smacked him in that smug little face."

My eyes filled with tears as my adopted dad described how he'd stood up for me. I thanked God for keeping His promise to me and sending angels to protect me. To Mr. Adama, I said, "Thank goodness you didn't hit him, sir; you're so big that you could have killed him."

"I know! I don't believe in violence under any circumstance, but he provoked me. I told him I used to respect him, but no more."

Mr. Adama sat down suddenly in his chair, his face sweating and his eyes moist and red. When he spoke again, his voice was soft and tender, like it had been when Mr. Mehu introduced us. "We'd better keep these things to ourselves for now," he told me. "I have no real power over E, but I promise you that no one is going to hurt you as long as I'm still in this place." He then gave me $50 and told me to buy something to take to the orphanage the next time I visited.

The very next day I received a call from the personnel office to tell me that, at Mr. Adama's request, I was being transferred to an office with an all-female supervisory staff. I would also be receiving a small pay raise. Mr. Adama was transferred to Somalia soon afterward, and a short time later, Mr. E was recalled by his government and left Rwanda.

Mr. Adama and I kept in touch for many years, and whenever we spoke, I was reminded that God reaches our hearts through His other children, and that angels really do walk among us.

The last I heard from my original surrogate father, Mr. Mehu, was in a letter several years ago when he moved away from America. He told me that he'd always think of me as his daughter, and at the end of the letter, he wrote: "Hold tight the gifts God has blessed you with; always keep your innocence and integrity."

CHAPTER 12

JOHN RETURNS

John was a young man I'd met during my first year of university. He was a few years older than I was and a good-looking, courteous, kind, and very persistent fellow.

We had mutual friends in Mataba, so John had a good reason to introduce himself to me one day; once he did, he was pretty much a fixture in my life. We enjoyed each other's company and talked for hours at a time during our long walks on campus. Like me, John believed that the most important things in life were a strong faith in God, a love of family, and a good education. Our biggest differences were that he was a Hutu and a Protestant—but for us, tribe wasn't an issue at all, and he respected how important Catholicism was to me. John and I were happily in love, and by my third year at school, we were talking about marriage. All that was left was to get our parents together for dinner so that we could make the big announcement.

Unfortunately, our love didn't survive the genocide.

The country exploded into murder so quickly that I didn't have time to write John—who was in Kigali—before I went into hiding. Because he was Hutu, I knew that he was probably safe, and I often wondered if he'd come looking for me after the killing started. Yet even though Pastor Murinzi was John's uncle, I hadn't had any word from or about my boyfriend during my first two months in the bathroom. Then one morning I heard his voice through the bathroom door. At first I thought that eight weeks without a proper meal had left me so weak I was hallucinating. But when I heard John's familiar laugh, I had no doubt that he was in the pastor's house and had come looking for me.

As it turned out, John didn't know I was at his uncle's, but had come to Mataba with three dozen of his Hutu relatives to escape the civil war raging around Kigali. They were afraid of being killed by Tutsi soldiers and knew that our province of Kibuye was a Hutu stronghold, where the government soldiers had been keeping the Tutsi rebels at bay. John had come to the pastor's for the same reason I had: to avoid being killed.

My spirits lifted, knowing that my boyfriend was near, and I was certain that Pastor Murinzi would sneak him in to visit me in the bathroom, which he did. The visit, however, was a disaster. When I saw John for the first time, I wanted to hug him to pieces. With some of the first words I'd spoken since being in hiding, I expressed how much I'd missed him and how hard I'd prayed for God to keep him safe.

But all the man who supposedly loved me could think to say was, "Ugh, you're so skinny, Immaculée! Hugging you is like holding a bag of bones!"

He didn't even tell me he was happy to see me alive, but instead declared he was glad I was still reasonably pretty after losing 40 pounds, and was relieved I hadn't been raped!

The genocide changed everyone's sense of priorities, and John was no exception. Over the next few weeks he all but ignored me, visiting once or twice and then only for a minute or two. I asked him to at least send me a note once in a while to let me know he was thinking about me while I was trapped in that little room, but he didn't send anything. To make matters worse, I could hear him laughing and playing soccer with his friends outside the house— he was having fun while I was hiding for my life and my people were being slaughtered!

Finally, just before the other women and I escaped to the French camp, John told me that he was glad I'd lost so much weight because other men wouldn't be attracted to a skeleton. "One less thing for me to worry about," he said.

What kind of love is this? I wondered. *It's not the kind, patient, and supportive love that the Bible tells us should exist between man and woman.*

When I left the pastor's house later that night, I left behind my future with John.

JOHN AND HIS FAMILY LEFT RWANDA TO AVOID THE CHAOS that followed the genocide, but they returned as soon as the new Tutsi government announced that innocent Hutus could come back to the country without fear of reprisal. He paid a surprise visit to me at the UN one afternoon after I'd finished work, and my heart skipped a beat when I saw him standing on the other side of the gate, waving at me. After all the loss and bloodshed, here was someone from my old life whom I'd loved.

"Thank God He has spared you," I told him when we were reunited. "I've prayed every day that you and your family would be safe."

"Immaculée, you look so much better now! You've put on a few pounds," John replied, hugging me. "Now that we've found each other, let's never be apart again. Promise you'll never leave me again!"

I was so overwhelmed by his outburst of affection that all I could say was, "It's good to see you, too."

As John walked me home to Sarah's, he told me everything he'd been through since leaving Rwanda. He'd been more fortunate than many Hutus who fled the country: John's father was a Protestant pastor whose church had ministerial ties across Africa, so the family had been able to find comfortable lodging while living in exile in Zaire, unlike the countless wretches who'd ended up in refugee camps.

"The worst part of leaving the country was what happened to us coming back," he remarked, telling me how Tutsi soldiers had stopped his family at the border and searched their car for weapons.

"I guess they were checking everybody to see if they were Interahamwe, but they treated us like we were all guilty—like we were killers—even though we hadn't done anything wrong. You know we didn't hurt anyone, don't you?" John was completely innocent, but like many innocent Hutus after the holocaust, the guilt he felt through tribal association sometimes made him feel as culpable as if he'd picked up a machete himself.

"Of course I know that," I answered truthfully. I knew John's entire family very well, and none of them were capable of harming another human being. John's youngest brother, Karame, had even been killed by the Interahamwe because he didn't support the genocide.

"When they didn't find any guns in the car, they started reading our old love letters I'd saved from school. Then they held up a picture of you and started laughing at me. They said, 'You're a Hutu—do you think a Tutsi woman is ever going to have anything to do with you after what your people did to us? She's gone; you can forget about her forever.' But that's not true, is it, Immaculée? I told them you wouldn't hate me for being Hutu. You and I are going to pick up where we left off, right?"

I didn't know how to react. Did he think that I'd tell him I loved him to prove the Tutsi soldiers wrong—to prove I didn't hate Hutus? It was crazy. I was happy to see John and glad to have a friend I could share my tears with, but he'd treated me so poorly while I was in hiding that I was sure I'd never be able to love him the way he wanted me to.

I've always found it difficult to end any kind of relationship, even with a girlfriend. And, from the desperate look in John's eyes, I knew I'd crush him if I rejected him at that moment. So instead of telling him that I didn't think we'd ever be able to get back to the way we were, I said, "You know what happened to my family, and my heart hasn't healed yet. I can't even think of being in a romance. There's too much pain for me to deal with right now, so you have to give me time to heal."

My family in front of our home in Mataba, two years before the genocide. In the back are four nuns from my father's school standing beside my dad and mom. In the front row, from left: family friend Claude, my brother Vianney, Marie (a novice nun), me, and my brothers Damascene and Aimable. Beside me on my left is my four-year-old goddaughter, Clarisse, who was murdered during the genocide.

My good friend Marianne (on the left) during our first year of high school. Marianne's family was killed in the genocide, and I haven't been able to locate her since.

My brother Vianney at age 17.

Me at age 13, not far from the hill where I planted flowers with Jeanette, hoping that the Virgin Mary would appear to us.

My brother Damascene with his girlfriend, Clarisse, three months before the genocide. He was going to ask her to marry him as soon as he'd saved enough from his teaching salary to buy a house. Clarisse was killed as well.

Hutu exodus: Tens of thousands of Hutu refugees crowd the road near Goma, Zaire (now the Congo), during the chaotic first days after the genocide. Fearing reprisal killings, they're heading east along the northern shore of Lake Kivu toward a refugee camp for exiled Rwandans. *[Photo courtesy of UNHCR, B. Press, July 1994]*

Victims of the cholera epidemic in the Munigi refugee camp near Goma. Cholera killed tens of thousands of Hutus who fled Rwanda into Zaire after the genocide. *[Photo courtesy of UNHCR, F. Loock, August 1994]*

Hutu exodus: Thousands of Hutu refugees waiting to cross into the Congo over the Ruzizi Bridge just south of Lake Kivu. Two million Hutus fled Rwanda after the genocide. *[Photo courtesy of UNHCR, H.J. Davies, August 1994]*

Return of the Hutu exodus: Hundreds of thousands of Hutu refugees returned en masse to Rwanda in late 1996 after more than two years in exile. Here, refugees pour into Rwanda from Tanzania at the Rusumo border crossing. *[Photo courtesy of UNHCR, H.J. Davies, December 1996]*

The skulls of Ntarama Church: More than 5,000 Tutsi parishioners were murdered while seeking shelter in this church, south of Kigali, which now serves as a memorial to the victims. Churches were among the worst killing fields during the genocide. *[Photo courtesy of Matthew Reichel]*

This is the gravesite of my mother, Marie Rose Kankindi, and my brother Damascene Jean Muhirwa. (My seven-year-old cousin, Rukundo, is also buried beside them.) Their bodies are resting in the ruins of our old home overlooking Lake Kivu.

KANKINDI ROSE
MUHIRWA J.D
RUKUNDO
BAZIZE ITSEMBABWOKO

1994

The view of Lake Kivu from the backyard of our family home in Mataba.

Taking a break at my United Nations job where I worked with UN volunteers from around the world. The trucks in the background carried supplies to the party we threw for the orphans at Mother Teresa's.

At Kigali International Airport in early 1995, on the first day of one of my early jobs at the United Nations. I was in charge of greeting UN employees arriving in the country and briefing them on Rwandan politics and culture.

At my wedding in 1998 with my friend Chantal, who paid for my wedding gown.

At my wedding with my friend Norah, who paid for all the food.

The cow Bryan brought to the wedding for the traditional dowry.

At my wedding. On the left is my father's friend Sayinzoga, who volunteered to host the ceremony at his Kigali home. With him are two of my dad's cousins, who returned to Rwanda after spending years living in exile in foreign countries.

Visiting Pastor Murinzi at his home near Mataba in 2004 with my children, Nikki and B.J. I'd returned to Rwanda to attend my brother Aimable's wedding; it was my first trip back since leaving in 1998.

Nikki and B.J. chasing cows and goats in a Matuba field, just as I did when I was growing up.

With my aunts at their home in Kibuye. From left: me, my aunts Jeanne and Esperance, three local girls, and a relative of ours named Jeannette (at the far right holding a baby). In front are a group of neighborhood children and my son, B.J. (on the far left), who is busy pulling apart my aunts' flower garden.

Cake for 200: The 2004 Christmas party we threw for the orphans at Mother Teresa's, I'm comforting a young boy who had just been fitted with a new leg brace.

At Aimable's wedding in December 2004, the first gathering of my extended family since the genocide ten years before. I'm in the middle, wearing the blue dress; my brother and his lovely bride, Sauda, are on my right. In front of me, with arms folded, is my daughter, Nikki, and two over from me on the left is Bryan, holding a restless B.J.

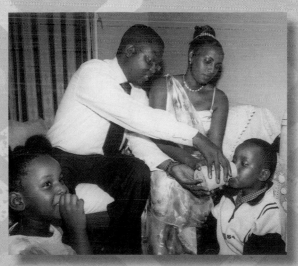

Aimable and Sauda after their wedding. Here, they're following tradition by sharing *Ikivuguto*, which is fresh buttermilk, with my children. The ritual signifies the importance of newlyweds nurturing the youngest members of the family and society.

My beautiful sister-in-law, Sauda, the sister I never had.

My cousin Ganza at Aimable's wedding. Not long after this picture was taken, Ganza was ordained as a Jesuit priest.

Freezing in America: This is my first winter (1998) in New York City, as well as my first experience with snow. I had yet to grasp the concept of wearing warm winter boots!

My sweet baby girl. Once Nikki's colic passed, she never stopped laughing and smiling.

A proud mother with a happy daughter.

Nikki and her little brother, B.J.. The two of them love being with each other and are best friends.

My wonderful kids, the joy of my life.

Nikki's first communion, at St. Clare's Parish in Queens, New York.

My cousin Ganza in a friend's backyard in upstate New York giving his first Mass in the United States. That's me in the foreground dancing with excitement. (Spring of 2008)

Visiting Belgium for a wedding in May 2008. On my right is my godfather, dear friend, and spiritual advisor, Father Jean Baptiste Bugingo; on my left is an old friend from the UN in Kigali, Alphonsine, with her husband, Antoine, and their two children Yannik (front left) and Angela.

A group of genocide survivors in Rwanda to whom I spoke about faith and forgiveness during a 2005 visit. I'm on the far right, facing away from the camera.

The statue of the Virgin Mary at Kibeho, which is becoming one of the most famous pilgrimage sites in Africa. Each year hundreds of thousands of people visit the shrine of Our Lady of Kibeho.

With a group of worshipers at Our Lady of Sorrows church in Kibeho. On my right is Anathalie, one of the visionaries visited by the Virgin Mary. Anathalie lives in Kibeho and spends her days spreading Mary's message of love, prayer, and peace.

With my dear friend Wayne Dyer, who helped bring my story to the world.

"So, maybe in a little while, Immaculée? Is that right? You just need a little time?"

"I don't know . . . maybe. Right now, the only one I can love freely is God."

FOR THE NEXT SEVERAL MONTHS, John regularly dropped by my work and home to visit. Sometimes we'd go for a walk, or a drive in his father's car. He kept asking me to go steady, but my heart wasn't available to him. It was more important for me to spend time with the orphans, or in prayer, than pretending to be in love. When John looked at me, he saw the girl he'd known before the genocide, and he wanted his old life back. But that life was gone, and it was never coming back.

As a friend, I wanted to help ease his suffering, so I tried to feel more for him than I actually did. Some nights when I went to sleep, I'd tell myself, "Tomorrow you will wake up and love John again." Yet it never happened.

I was still grieving for my parents and brothers and couldn't imagine what it would be like to cuddle with, kiss, or even just hold hands with someone. When I made this plain to John, he got angry and said, "Your family weren't the only ones to die, Immaculée. Lots of people lost someone they loved. It's been months now; get over them already!"

I couldn't believe what was coming out of his mouth. Had the massacre of Tutsis become so commonplace in our country that others, even those I was close to, thought it was something we'd just "get over"?

"I will never be *over* them, John!" I cried. "How can you think like that? We're talking about my *family*. The genocide wasn't a movie—I can't get up and walk away from it after a couple of hours! This is going to be part of me for the rest of my life. We are all going to be affected by this forever, so we have to support each other and try to understand our feelings. We can't just forget it happened."

"No, that's exactly what we should do. We should forget it happened at all."

"That's never going to be possible! We have to forgive the people who did it, but we are never, ever going to forget."

The rift between John and me was something I often saw in Rwanda after the genocide. Some Hutus would just as soon have put the past behind them and act as if the holocaust had never happened, which only inflamed Tutsi resentment and anger.

That night I went to my little room at the Christus Center and prayed for God to ease my old friend's suffering, but I knew that it was up to John to seek God's help on his own. For my part, I asked the Lord to help me continue to lead the life He wanted me to lead: "If I'm meant to be with John, I know You will open my heart to him when the time is right. I trust in You."

God truly has many ways of reaching us. For example, when I looked up after praying, I saw the answer to my trouble with John right in front of me—stitched into the quilted wall-hanging that had stared at me for months: "Behind every story of true love, there is a story of great patience." I knew that, with patience, a great love story would unfold in Rwanda, that God would bring Hutus and Tutsis together through forgiveness.

Unfortunately, my old boyfriend couldn't be patient.

FOR SOME REASON, JOHN THOUGHT I COULDN'T LOVE HIM because I was holding on too tightly to the love I had for my family. Therefore, he hated the red and white rosary my father had given me before I went into hiding. That rosary had acted as a lifeline for me during the genocide and was the only thing of my father's that I owned—every time I prayed using those beads, I felt him beside me. I absolutely treasured that rosary.

"You love this thing more than you love me!" John yelled one evening when he'd come to see me at the UN. He grabbed my hand roughly, pried the beads from my fingers, and continued, "Maybe if I get rid of it, you'll run out of reasons not to marry me." And he walked away with my most prized possession.

I shouted at John that if he didn't return my rosary, I'd never speak to him again. That night, he left a bruise on my wrist—and on my heart. When I got to Sarah's, I lay in bed and cried for hours, feeling as if my father had been taken away from me all over again.

"Immaculée, this relationship is no good for you. Why don't you dump him and be done with it?" my dear friend asked, after trying to console me most of the night.

"Because he's hurting so much . . . I don't want to hurt him any more."

"Don't feel too bad for him," she retorted, and then shared with me something he'd let slip to her the day before. "John said he wished you'd died in the genocide so he could suffer properly, the way everyone else is. He told me that he doesn't want to suffer because you're alive and might fall in love with another man instead of him."

Her words stunned me—how could someone who claimed to love me wish that I were dead? All I could figure was that he must have been in terrible pain to say such a thing. When I told Sarah that, she just shook her head at me.

John returned my father's rosary a few days later. But the following week, we went to a friend's wedding together, and I left my purse with him while I chatted with the bride. When I returned, the rosary was gone from my purse. John denied taking it, but I knew he had. I never saw my father's rosary again.

I moped around the house for days mourning my loss until Sarah's mom finally took me aside and gave me some advice I'd never forget: "Immaculée, I wouldn't be surprised if your father played a part in making that rosary disappear. He wanted you to use it to reach God, not as something to cherish for itself, like it was some kind of precious jewel. The value of the rosary is in your heart and in its prayer, not in the beads." Taking her own rosary and pressing it into my hand, she said, "Use this one, and if you get too attached to it, give it away and find another. If you keep your father's memory in your heart, nobody will be able to steal it."

At that moment I knew my father's rosary would always be with me—its shape, its colors, and its texture would be safe in my soul. I knew what God wanted me to do: focus on prayer, not on material things. John may have tried to hurt me by taking away a possession

I prized, but he'd given me a more precious gift, and I forgave him. As Mother Teresa said, understanding all is forgiving all.

John came to the house on a Saturday morning not long after to try to patch things up. When I opened the door, I could see he wasn't doing so well; his eyes had dark circles and he'd lost weight. However, I told him, "It's probably better not to see each other, as my feelings haven't changed."

He pleaded with me to take a drive in the country with him so we could settle everything nicely. "Just as friends," he promised.

Sarah was standing behind the door, shaking her head and whispering, "Don't go with him, Immaculée. He said he wanted you dead!" But the man standing before me didn't look dangerous; he looked like he could use a friend. So I told her I'd be back for supper and headed out the door.

As we left Kigali, John said that he wanted to drive to Butare and visit our old university campus. "Maybe if we return to where we loved each other so much, those old feelings will come back," he explained earnestly.

What happened to "just as friends"? I wondered. Aloud, I said, "John, Butare is three or four hours away, and there's still a lot of killing along the roads—maybe it's not safe."

"It will be fine," he assured me. We were driving up a very steep hill when he began to lay out his plans for our future, beginning with my quitting my job.

"What do you mean . . . why would I do that? Do you know what it took to get that job? Do you know how much money I send to my aunts and cousins every month? What on earth are you talking about?"

"I don't want you working when we're married," he replied. "It wouldn't be right. If you move in with my parents and me, you won't need extra money, and then we can get married later."

"First of all, I would never move in with you without getting married, and I've told you my heart is not ready for marriage. I'm still healing."

"I don't want to hear about your hurting heart anymore, Immaculée!" John exclaimed. "That's all you ever talk about.

Everybody is hurting in Rwanda—it's time to go back to how we used to be before any of this happened!"

"We *can't* go back, John!"

We'd reached the top of the hill, and he twisted the steering wheel hard to the left and veered toward the edge, less than 30 feet away. "If we can't live together, we'll die together," he said, more calmly now. "I want this pain to end."

He accelerated toward the cliff.

"John, I have faced far worse than this, and God has always protected me!" I shouted. "My soul is safe, but if you drive over this cliff, you will be committing a terrible sin. You are a good person . . . don't risk going to hell because you're angry!"

John slammed his foot on the brake, which caused the car to skid along until its front wheels went over the side of the cliff. The undercarriage dropped to the ground with a bang, and the car stopped moving forward. The motor sputtered and died, and the front half of the vehicle was sticking out in midair. Through the side window, all I could see were the rocks 40 feet below. The metal chassis groaned as the car teetered slowly forward, then back.

I placed my hands on the dashboard, trying to push myself away from the edge, and John simply rested his forehead on the steering wheel. We sat in silence until he finally started the engine and carefully backed up to the road. We drove back to Kigali without saying a word.

The next time I'd see John would be when he told me he was planning to leave the country.

The next morning, I really needed to go to Mass and have a long talk with God. While walking to church, I ran into one of John's old friends from university, a Tutsi named Jaffe who'd escaped to Burundi during the genocide. He'd always been very friendly with me at school, but now he greeted me with a hard voice—no smile, no hello.

"Immaculée, I hear that you're dating John again. Is that true?"

"John is my friend— "

Jaffe cut me off before I could say anything else. *"Friend!* I can't believe you're seeing a Hutu after what they've done. What kind of Tutsi sister are you?"

"You're John's friend, Jaffe, and you know that he's a good person who didn't hurt anyone."

"I don't have Hutu friends, Immaculée. You may think that man didn't hurt anyone, but he's a Hutu, and that makes him guilty. You know, some of our Tutsi schoolmates joined the RPF and fought the Hutus . . . when they heard about John, they said they'd kill him before they'd let him marry you. But I think killing him would be too easy. If I ever see you two together again, I'll go to the court and accuse him of murdering Tutsis. It doesn't matter if he's innocent or guilty—he'll rot in prison for ten years before he gets a trial . . . if he lives that long," Jaffe warned, staring at me fiercely.

The jails were already overflowing with thousands and thousands of accused Hutu killers, and hundreds more were being arrested every week. The majority of Tutsi judges and lawyers had been murdered in the holocaust, and trials were years away for most. Jaffe's threat was very real.

"You know John is innocent," I told him. "You can't accuse an innocent person of murder."

"There are no innocent Hutus."

"That's a lie, and bearing false witness is a sin against God."

"God! There *is* no God in this country anymore, Immaculée. The only justice we Tutsis get is the one we make for ourselves. Remember that when you pick your friends."

Jaffe walked away, leaving me more uncertain about our nation's future than ever before. First, John had accused me of not loving him because he was Hutu, and now Jaffe was accusing me of not being a good Tutsi because I cared for a Hutu. And if people in the new government thought as Jaffe did, how long would it be before there was another genocide—this time against Hutus? If people convinced themselves that God had left Rwanda and then chose to seek justice through false accusations and vengeance, the cycle of violence that plagued Rwanda would never end.

At church, I prayed for Jaffe: *Take the pain and hatred from his heart, Lord. Show him that You are with him, that You are with all of us . . . show him that You didn't leave our country. And please guide our leaders and help them bring us a future of peace. Let them be ruled by justice, not vengeance.*

I also asked God to watch over John and his family, praying that our Hutu-Tutsi friendship in this angry country had not put their lives or freedom at risk. And finally, I asked Him to take away the burden of my relationship with John, and to protect him from false accusations and arrest: *Thank You for stopping him from hurting us on the cliff, God, but as You can see, things are very bad. I don't know what to do . . . any decision I make will hurt him, so please help me do the right thing. We both need Your help now . . . perhaps it's time You sent John away from Rwanda for his own good. Amen.*

Before I left, I opened my Bible for inspiration, turning to one of my favorite psalms. "Cast your cares on the Lord and he will sustain you," it reminded me. "He will never let the righteous fall."

A few days later, John came to Sarah's with news that his father had been called to Zambia to preach, so the family was making preparations to leave Rwanda within the week.

"I don't know, Immaculée. I don't want to lose you forever, but maybe it's a good decision," he said, looking to me to make up his mind.

I thought about what Jaffe had said and knew that John would never survive in prison. This seemed to be God's way of answering my prayer. "Yes, John," I responded. "If you think it's better for you to go to Zambia, then you should go."

He searched my face with his sad eyes and then walked away. I scolded myself for not telling him plainly that we were not meant to be, and that I *wanted* him to go to Zambia to start a new life and find the happiness we'd never find with each other. But again, I'd been afraid of hurting him further and didn't answer him the way I should have.

God must not have been happy with my answer either, for that evening He put me in a situation where I had no choice but to tell John the truth of my heart. It began when he asked me to meet him for a farewell cup of tea at the house of my friend Aloise. This struck me as a bit odd, but I thought it would be wise to say our good-byes with someone else in the room.

The three of us were chatting pleasantly in Aloise's living room when the front door suddenly burst open and half a dozen people marched in, including two of John's brothers and my friend DeeDee.

"What's going on?" I asked.

No one said anything until John stood up and announced, "I've asked you all to come here because you're either my friends or Immaculée's friends. I want you to witness what she says when I ask her to tell me the truth."

Everyone then formed a semicircle in front of me, with John in the center. "Okay, I need an answer," he said. "If I move to Zambia with my parents, I may never come back. So, before I decide to leave Rwanda forever, I want to know if we're going to get married. Just answer me this one question, Immaculée: Are you in love with me? Yes or no?"

I wanted to be angry for being set up for questioning as though I were a criminal, but John looked so wounded that I couldn't be mad. My heart was racing; everyone was staring at me so intensely that I thought their eyes would burn through me. I wanted my mother to defend me, and to have the rest of my family there for support. I didn't want to hurt John, but I didn't know how to avoid it either.

"Well, you mean a lot to me, and I care about what happens to you," I said.

"That's not what I asked. Are you or are you not in love with me?"

"Answer him, Immaculée. You've been leading this boy on too long," Aloise chimed in.

"Answer," echoed one of John's cousins, whom I'd never met.

"Yes or no," John demanded.

"All right then . . . no!" I blurted out. "No, John. I don't love you, and I'm not *in* love with you. You're a friend, and that's all it will ever be. But please don't be hurt—you're a good person, and there will be someone else for you. Maybe there's someone waiting in Zambia for you . . ."

I felt as if I'd stabbed my old friend. John started to cry, his brothers and cousins whisked him from the room and out of the house, and Aloise pushed her wheelchair into her bedroom without saying good-bye to me.

I looked up at DeeDee, the only one who was on my side. She smiled, took my hand, and said, "Don't feel bad, Immaculée. They asked you for the truth, and that's what you gave them."

WHEN I WENT TO BED THAT NIGHT, I WAS SO UPSET by what I'd said to John that I forgot to pray. I cried for the hurt I had caused him and wondered if my heart would ever be able to love romantically again. If that was how it had to be, so be it—I'd give my heart to God and my love to the orphans. I sobbed until I fell asleep, and then I had the most amazing dream.

I was back in Aloise's living room sitting in the same chair, but this time my legs were chained at the ankles, and my arms were tied behind my back with tight leather straps. John and the others were standing around me wearing long wooden masks and thrusting spears at my chest.

Suddenly my mother appeared, floating down from the ceiling in a white flowing dress. She hovered above the floor, between me and the sharp tips of the spears. As she turned her face toward me and smiled, the chains fell from my legs, and the bindings dropped from my arms. Then Mom spoke to me, her voice as gentle as it had been when I was a child and she sang to me.

"Don't ever think you're alone, Immaculée. Your mother is always with you . . . I am always watching over you." She turned to the others, who dropped their spears and backed away. "Give my daughter peace," she told them, "and let her travel her own path. If she needs advice, it will come from someone who loves her—it will come from her mother, not from you."

When I awoke in the morning, I felt freer than I had in months. I was no longer troubled by my old boyfriend's expectations or anguish. The truth had been told, and it had set us both free.

John came to say good-bye the day he moved to Zambia. We shook hands and wished each other well. He told me he was sorry if he'd hurt me and forgave me for any pain I'd caused him. I told him the same thing. We parted as friends, and I was happy when I later heard that he'd fallen in love and gotten married. If John and I could move forward positively, then other Hutus and Tutsis who had fallen out with each other would be able to do the same.

I felt my heart beginning to heal, and that gave me hope that our country could heal as well.

CHAPTER 13

AN ARMY OF LOVE

From atop the high hill above Mother Teresa's, Kigali still looked like a military base more than two years after the war had ended. The heavy rumbling of passing tanks rose from the streets below, and I could see a long line of armored personnel carriers snaking through the city, transporting RPF troops to fight Hutu insurgents along the Zairian border. There were soldiers stationed outside every government building, and driving across the city meant passing through several military checkpoints.

Every time I crested that hill on my way to the orphanage, I wondered, *What would I do if I could command all those soldiers for a day?*

"What could *we* do with an army, Lord? What war could we fight with love instead of guns?" I asked Him out loud, navigating the loose red dirt as I descended the road toward Mother Teresa's. I often chatted with God and asked Him questions while walking the hills of Kigali, and sometimes, as on this occasion, He answered right away. In front of the orphanage's blue metal gates, two soldiers were dropping off a group of children they'd picked up on the street. A light flashed in my mind: *If I had an army, I'd bring it here to fight for the orphans*. Of course I didn't have an army, but I knew where I could get one.

I BEGAN WORKING AS AN ASSISTANT TO THE VOLUNTEER COORDINATOR for the United Nations Development Programme (UNDP) in the middle of 1996. I loved the job because so many people I worked with had come to Rwanda following their hearts. They weren't there for money or to advance their careers but because they genuinely wanted to help.

Every year countless kind souls assembled in selected regions to celebrate volunteerism by joining forces to complete a formidable community project in less than 24 hours—usually along the lines of digging a well, repairing a road, or building a house. It was a lot of hard work and heavy lifting, so I thought what better work could there be than lifting the spirits of 200 orphans for a day?

I decided that the UN would supply me with an army of volunteers, and our battleground would be Mother Teresa's. While the celebration, known as the International Volunteer Day (IVD), is a global event and a very big deal at the United Nations, my problem was that I was just an assistant and one of the lowest-ranking employees in my department. I had no voice at all in policy or planning, yet somehow I had to convince my boss, at least ten staff members, and the top UN officials in Europe that a group of Kigali orphans was as important as a village well or an irrigation ditch. But I believed that God had put this idea into my head for a reason, and I knew that I'd better follow through.

The IVD was a month away, and I still had a few days before the first scheduled planning-committee meeting. Although part of my job involved setting up the committee meetings, my boss, Coulibaly, hadn't been invited to attend. That was the first thing I had to change—if I could have my voice heard, I was sure that I could convince everybody to accept my idea.

Coulibaly was the most disheveled, disorganized, absent-minded supervisor I'd ever had. One time he had three of us running around the office looking for an urgent fax he'd received from the world headquarters in New York City. He insisted that someone had taken it from his desk, but after tearing the office apart, he discovered that he'd been sitting on the important document all morning. Despite his scattered work methods, Coulibaly was perhaps the most hardworking and productive person at the UNDP. He was also sweet, funny, and deeply passionate about our country's recovery.

Originally from Mali, Coulibaly had come to Rwanda as a student. He fell in love with the country and with a young Rwandan woman, and he'd remained devoted to both for the past 30 years. I knew he couldn't accept an IVD proposal that hadn't been tabled at an official meeting, so I asked him for a favor.

"Coulibaly, would it be all right if I sat in on the IVD planning committee tomorrow? I'm interested in seeing how senior staff decides on proposals."

"As long as you bring chocolates," my boss teased. He had a sweet tooth and was known for walking around the office with fistfuls of candy. More than once he'd forgotten about the treats he was carrying around and had shown up at a staff meeting with his face and clothing covered in melted chocolate.

"I'll bring a box," I agreed with a smile, and then went home to finish preparing my presentation. I'd been scribbling ideas in a notebook for days, sketching out activities for volunteers and children, listing repair jobs that were needed at the orphanage, and organizing the tools and supplies required for the day. The nuns at Mother Teresa's had approved my plan earlier in the week, but we'd agreed not to tell the children about it until I received the go-ahead.

The meeting the next morning would be the first time I'd pitched an idea at the United Nations. The more I thought about it, the more nervous I became. I looked at the notes I'd made in my book:

Soda: *15 cases*
Rice: *10 bags*
Beans: *8 sacks*
Cakes: *25*
Paint: *30 gallons*
Blackboards: *10*
Coloring books: *250*
Medicine: *alcohol swabs, bandages, disinfectant*

What I had thought was a thorough and professional presentation now resembled a grade-schooler's wish list for a class picnic. *I'm going to look like an idiot!* I thought, in a burst of panic. *These people are coming from all over Africa thinking that they're going to build shelters, not sit around with kids and crayons. They're going to laugh me out of the office!*

Sarah and her sister were away visiting relatives for the weekend, and I had the bedroom to myself. So I got on my knees and prayed out loud: "Did I just imagine that You wanted me to do this, Lord? Am I looking for signs from You where none exist? As always, I'm putting my trust in You. You brought me to these children in the first place, so please help me bring something special to them now. Help me show them that there is love and caring for them in the world. Take my nervousness from me—I don't mind looking like a fool if I'm a fool for You. Please be with me when I speak for the orphans tomorrow, and touch my voice. Thank You . . . and I'll see You at the office tomorrow morning!"

The meeting started at 9 A.M., and I made sure I was there an hour early to type up my proposal on the computer and make printed copies. *Now that's professional,* I thought.

There were a dozen coordinators from half a dozen African nations in the room when Coulibaly walked in and requested proposals, saying, "So, let's hear what you've all got. Who wants to go first?"

No one spoke. People looked at each other and around the room, and then they shrugged their shoulders and smiled sheepishly.

"What? Nobody has anything?" Coulibaly asked incredulously. "Come on, people—we have two weeks before the IVD, and nobody has a single idea? This is going to be a big deal at headquarters, so you better come up with something fast, and it better be good."

"Maybe we could do something at a school this year? Students are starting to come back, so we could repair some classrooms, maybe build a new schoolhouse . . . something with schools," offered Martine, a volunteer from Guinea.

140

"Well . . . *something* to do with schools. Okay, that's good, but not very specific. Come on now, it's a little country, but it's got a lot of problems. It's not that hard to find something to fix, people."

"How about building a clinic in a village?" another volunteer suggested. "So many people are walking around with infections and sores, but they can't go anywhere to get treated."

"Sure," Coulibaly replied, "a clinic is a possibility. Decide which province, locate a village, and then let's see some research, for heaven's sake. I can't believe that none of you has explored an idea. I expect developed proposals from everybody by the end of the week, so if no one has anything else . . ."

"I have an idea, sir," I said, jumping up as Coulibaly stood to leave. I looked at him hopefully, laying my neatly stacked pile of freshly printed proposals on the desk.

Coulibaly looked surprised but pleased. He'd never heard me speak up at a meeting before, and my sudden boldness amused him. "Okay, Immaculée, what have you got?"

The entire group was staring at me, since local Rwandan hires did not suggest policies and programs. We filled out requisition forms, copied documents, greeted guests, and performed other low-level duties; we never encroached upon the staff's jurisdiction. The UN was quite territorial in that there was a rigid hierarchy, and everyone knew his or her place.

I cleared my throat and launched timidly into my presentation. "Um, well, I thought it would be nice if the volunteers spent the day at Mother Teresa's orphanage right here in Kigali. There are 200 boys and girls living there whose parents were killed in the genocide, or whose mothers were raped during the war. I thought we could start by taking food and drinks to the kids and—"

"Forget it, we don't do orphans," Kokou interrupted. He was a tall, skinny man from Togo, and one of the more haughty and disagreeable staff members.

"But why not?" I asked, not wanting to be shut down before I even had a chance to make my case. "Those children are as much a part of the community as anyone else, and they need more help than most. They have absolutely nothing."

"Are you crazy?" he retorted. "People are coming here from all over the continent to work on a development project. That is what we do here—*international development.* This is the UNDP, not a babysitting service."

"You have a nice idea, Immaculée, but Kokou is right about the development aspect," Coulibaly said sympathetically. "We've got to think about sustainability. We need a project that will keep giving to the community after we've left."

"That's exactly what I'm proposing, sir. I've thought about this quite a bit. These children are the first generation to follow the genocide; they *are* Rwanda's sustainable resource. They're the ones who will be rebuilding the country, and we need to give them as much good soil to grow in as we can. We can't let them fall by the wayside. If we can show them that they're loved by so many people, it will give them something to hope for. I know it doesn't sound like much, but one special day could give them something that could last a lifetime. Honestly, just one day of love could make a world of difference for them."

"We're here to provide aid and technical support to the community, Immaculée. I've never seen the word *love* in the UNDP mandate," Kokou snickered.

"Well, look at my proposal," I said. "Everything I've put down here is part of our mandate. We can spend the day teaching them to read numbers and letters so they can recognize signs—that comes under the literacy program. We can treat their cuts and sores with the medication we bring—that's under the health program. And we can feed them the best meal they've had in two years—that's part of the food program. We can sing and dance with them— that's cultural development. And for community improvement, we can plant trees and flowers, clean and paint the building, make sure their water supply is clean—"

"Which is all a waste of resources," Kokou snapped. "Why would we throw away our one big day of the year doing something that will be gone the minute we leave?"

"But it *won't* be gone," I protested. "Not if we go there with love. We can show them there is a brighter world; we can inspire them."

"That's not our job," he said flatly.

"Yes, it is; that's exactly our job," argued Joelle, a young woman from Cameroon who was flipping through my proposal. "We are a humanitarian relief agency before anything else. Immaculée's right—who needs more relief than the orphans of genocide?"

"She's also right about our mandate," Martine added. "Everything in this proposal is part of a program we support. And she has the whole day planned out with a complete itinerary ready to go. I think it's a perfect idea."

"So do I," Joelle agreed.

I could feel my heart swelling as my proposal was passed around the table.

"You might be onto a really good idea here," Coulibaly told me, beaming with pride. "I think everyone here is going to go for it, even Kokou. Send the proposal off to headquarters in Germany. If they approve it, then we're going to the orphanage."

I sent off the proposal right away, but I didn't have to wait for an answer. I knew that God had already given His approval.

JUST BEFORE DAWN ON A BEAUTIFUL, WARM DECEMBER MORNING, more than 100 volunteers from Africa, Europe, America, Asia, and Australia gathered outside the UNDP office to receive their assignments. They loaded crates of food and drink into pickup trucks; tied giant blackboards on the roofs of minivans; and loaded boxes of coloring books, crayons, lesson guides, and notepads wherever there was space. We had wheelbarrows and crates filled with paint and tools, medical supplies, and recorded music for dancing.

Look at them all, Lord—Your army of love going into battle! I thought.

"Anything you want me to tell them before we head out, Immaculée?" Coulibaly asked.

"Just that they can't do this halfway—you can't fool an orphan by pretending to care. Whatever we do today, it has to come from the heart."

Before the convoy left for Mother Teresa's, Coulibaly called everyone together in a big circle around him and said, "What we're doing today is going to be different from what we normally do. These are little children who have experienced terrible things, so we have to make sure that we're sensitive and caring. Everything we do today has to be done with love—no half measures. Now let's go make some kids smile!"

It was one of the most joyful days I've ever had. The volunteers poured through the gates of the orphanage and were greeted by 200 singing children who had been waiting to welcome them. Someone set up a stereo and began playing traditional folk music, and several of the female Rwandan volunteers began teaching the older girls some of our country's dances. We set up the blackboards for reading lessons and gathered the children into circles to hear folk stories from around the world. We passed out the coloring books and crayons, and I told them to let their imaginations run free.

Half the group kept busy with the kids, while the rest divided up into work crews, patching and painting the walls, scrubbing floors and toilets, clearing rubbish and broken glass from the yard, and planting flowerbeds around the gates. By midafternoon, Mother Teresa's was sparkling like a jewel, and I'd never seen the orphans so happy.

The only upsetting incident for me was when I saw Aurea, a Tutsi woman I worked with at the UN, shove a toddler she'd been cuddling from her lap to the ground. The child sat silently in the dirt for a moment, registering what had happened, then began wailing.

"What happened, Aurea? Why did you drop her?" I asked, lifting the little one into my arms.

"Look at its nose, Immaculée."

"What are you talking about?"

"Its nose is flat. That baby is a Hutu."

I was so angry that I wanted to slap her. "How could you, Aurea? This is an innocent child; she can't even walk yet, and you hate her? For what? She hasn't harmed anyone!"

"I know. I'm sorry, Immaculée, but you know how hard it is . . . they killed my father and my brothers . . . I just can't hold her."

I sat beside Aurea and put the toddler back on her lap. "Hold that child like she is your own," I said, "because she *is* your own. That little girl belongs to all of us."

I sat with them until they were both smiling—the child's smile was real, and I hoped Aurea's was as well.

At the end of the day, a crew from the UN's radio station arrived at the orphanage to interview Coulibaly about why Mother Teresa's had been selected as Rwanda's IVD project.

"Talk to *her*," my boss said, pointing at me.

I'd never given a radio interview before. Despite the recording device and big microphone that the reporter waved in front of me, it didn't occur to me that what I was saying would be broadcast across the nation.

"Tell us why an orphanage was chosen to highlight the importance of volunteering in Rwanda," the reporter prompted me.

For the next ten minutes I said everything I could to praise the work of the volunteers who had come to my country from all over the world, and why I thought it was important for all of us to give back to our communities. "But the reason we came to Mother Teresa's is because these children are the ones who will build the new Rwanda," I said. "If we don't invest in their future, we won't have a future."

The next day I received messages at work from people from all over who'd heard my interview; my aunts even spent money to call me from Kibuye. "Immaculée! Immaculée!" Esperance hollered across the phone line. "You were on the radio! Everybody is talking about you. Everybody is going to the orphanages here with books and clothes. How did you do that? How did you manage to make all of Rwanda hear you?"

Of course, the answer could be summed up in one word: *God.*

❖ ❖

CHAPTER 14

BEES AND BLESSINGS

The second anniversary of the genocide had come and gone. While I was still missing my parents and brothers terribly, my heart was slowly awakening from its long months of mourning. For the first time, memories of Mom, Dad, Damascene, and Vianney kindled a feeling within me to start a family of my own. I'd asked God to bring me a good man when the time was right, and when I met Bryan Black at the UN, I knew I was finally ready for a relationship.

Bryan had joined the United Nations many years earlier and had come to Rwanda to help set up security for the new International Criminal Tribunal for Rwanda—the ICTR—based in Arusha, Tanzania. When we met in the spring of 1996, I was taken by his nice looks, charm, and easy Trinidadian manner. But most important, he shared my faith.

When we got to know each other better, we drove down to Mataba, where I introduced him to my aunts and cousins and showed him the ruins of my childhood home, including the gravesite of my mother and brother.

Bryan said that he couldn't fathom the pain of losing so many loved ones at one time—he himself had 14 siblings, all of whom were healthy and well. And he didn't push me for details about what I'd been through during the genocide, which was good, because talking about one sorrow could unleash all of my heartache.

When my brothers and I were children, our mother used a Rwandan saying to instruct us about why we must treat orphans gently. "Ukubita imfubyi ntuyibwiriza kurira," she'd say, which means: "When you beat an orphan, you don't have to beg her to cry—her tears will flow from a life full of sorrow." A good example of this was how I felt after a major argument I had with Bryan one morning when Sarah and her family were gone from the house, over something that I can't even remember now but was hugely important to me at the time. Our voices were raised in anger, when he suddenly stopped arguing and walked out the door, slamming it behind him.

I'm sure that many couples have similar quarrels during courtship, but for me, love was too painfully tied to loss and separation for such a disagreement not to have an impact. Bryan had left so abruptly that I thought he might never come back, which was exactly what had happened with my parents and brothers. I began to cry inconsolably. At first my tears fell because of Bryan, but the more I wept, the more I thought of my lost family. My mind was tortured with graphic images of their last moments of life—their cries of misery; the fear and desperation they felt facing the killers and knowing that there would be no mercy; the machetes; the horrible wounds; the blood. It was too much, too much!

Oh God, please take this pain from me. I can't bear it again!

I curled up on my bed in a fetal ball of anguish, crying out for my mother: "Mom, why did you leave me? Why, why, why?"

But the more frantically I wailed, the less I heard my own voice, for my sobs were drowned out by a buzzing around my head. The back of my neck tingled; I thought that someone had come into the room, so I instinctively rolled on my back to see if anyone was there. And there above me was a swarm of bees, swirling slowly down from the ceiling toward my face. The window was closed and the door shut, so I had no idea how they got there.

I panicked for a moment, worried that I was about to be stung, but then my body completely relaxed. The bees' low humming soothed my suffering like a lullaby, and they came so close that I could feel the tiny breeze created by their wings brushing my damp cheeks. I felt as though my mother had knelt down beside me and softly caressed my face with her hand. Her love encased me, and I knew that the insects would do me no harm . . . somehow, they'd brought my mom to me.

I closed my eyes and let my mind drift back to a summer afternoon during my childhood in Mataba, just after my mother had told my older brothers and our houseboy, Kaza, to take me with them to get the cooking water for our evening meal. I was 12 years old and had to walk double-time to keep up with Aimable, Damascene, and Kaza as they grabbed their buckets and headed out the door. The freshest water in our area came from a valley spring at the bottom of the steepest hill in the area—it was so high that it seemed more like a mountain to me.

This is what it must be like to be a bird, I thought when I reached the top of the hill. As I peered over the edge, the people down below were so far away that they looked like ants. The way down was treacherous: a narrow switchback trail zigzagged so precariously that even goats sometimes lost their footing and fell. My brothers and I were pretty familiar with the paths, though, and could usually get down to the stream within half an hour.

We were about halfway down when a swarm of honeybees rose from a bush just off the path; hovered over our heads in a dark, vibrating cloud; and then sailed away, looking like a dwindling black dot against the blue sky.

Once we reached the spring, Kaza and I filled our buckets and waited for my brothers in the shade, dangling our feet in the cool water. "I bet those bees made an awful lot of honey," he said.

"I love honey."

"Me, too. Where do you think the bees went?"

"They went so high that I bet they flew all the way to Zaire!"

"Then they'll be gone for a long time. Let's empty one of our buckets and go steal their honey on the way home."

"You're smart, Kaza."

My brothers joined us, and Damascene asked why one of the buckets was empty.

"We're going to fill it with honey," I answered.

"Are you crazy? Did you see all those bees?"

"They flew away," Kaza insisted.

"There must have been a thousand bees; they didn't all fly away," Aimable pointed out. To me, he said, "Forget about the honey. Go fill your bucket with water and we'll see you and Kaza back at the house."

The boys began climbing the hill, and Kaza and I stayed in the shade until they were far up the trail.

"Still want to get the honey, Immaculée?"

"Of course! I love honey, and so do my brothers. When they see how much I bring home, they'll beg me to give them some."

Kaza and I went to the bush where we saw the bees, and he knelt down with the empty bucket and pushed back the lowest branches.

"Ouch!" he yelled, quickly pulling his hand back and dropping the bucket into the bush. "It stung me! It stung me!" he cried, as a red welt erupted across his wrist.

When I tried to recover the bucket, a knot of bees the size of a watermelon shot out of the bush, hung in the air for a couple of seconds, and then hurtled straight at us.

"Run!" shouted Kaza, who was ten feet up the hill before I could turn around.

The first stinger burned into my upper lip like a sizzling spit of hot oil from my mom's black skillet. "Ohh . . . ," I whimpered, and before I could yell out, my face and neck exploded in bursts of searing pain. I covered my eyes and stumbled blindly for the path, but I only succeeded in falling into the bush and on top of the bees.

"Mom! *Mom!*" I shrieked, jumping up, falling, getting up, and running and falling again. "Mom! Oh, Mommy!" Even though I was lying facedown on the rocks now, waving my hands wildly around my ears in an attempt to fend off the attack that wouldn't stop, I continued to scream for my mother.

I heard Mom's name being exclaimed from above, and when I looked up toward the top of the hill, I heard my own name. A group of neighbors was trying to tell me to run, but I couldn't move. They shouted again for my mother to come: "Rose! Rose! Your daughter is in trouble! The bees have her!"

"Somebody help her!" yelled my mother, who was now at the top of the hill herself. "Why are you just standing there? My child is dying . . . help her!" Yet no one would come to me, since they were all afraid of the bees.

"I'm coming, Immaculée!" Mom called out, jumping off the edge of the hill and landing hard against the craggy pile of rocks below. She was wrapped up tightly in a traditional Rwandan dress that made walking difficult, so she lost her footing as soon as she reached the path. She crawled for a few feet in the dirt and then pushed herself upright.

"Come back, Rose! The bees will kill you!" the neighbors shouted.

My mom ignored them and ran along the rocky path, continuing to scream, "I'm coming, Immaculée! I'm coming!"

My mother's health was often fragile. She was so allergic to dust that walking the path to her job at the village schoolhouse could trigger a severe asthma attack, and she'd get winded climbing a short flight of stairs. But there she was—falling, rolling, and sliding down that dangerous decline to reach me.

I've never felt as loved by another person as I did at that moment, watching Mom through my swollen, bee-stung eyes as she threw herself headlong into the rocks and dust to come to my rescue. Even through my pain, I worried that she'd suffer a fatal asthma attack trying to reach me. I pulled myself up and ran to her so that she wouldn't have to come any farther down the hill and put herself in more danger.

She locked her arms around me, lifted me into the air, and began climbing toward the house, crying, "Thank God you're alive! Oh, thank God! I was so scared you would die and leave me. Oh God, I couldn't live without my child. I couldn't live if I lost my only daughter!" Her lungs crackled and wheezed as she rushed me upward to safety.

"It's okay, Mom, you can put me down. I can walk. It's okay . . . please, Mom, your asthma . . . put me down."

We stopped and sat on the rocks together for a few minutes while she caught her breath, and we were both sobbing. My face was badly swollen and ached horribly, but I didn't care about the pain. I hugged her, and she hugged me back. Then she took my hand and we walked together the rest of the way up the hill past our neighbors, who were speechless at having witnessed such a display of motherly love.

My mother's heroism that day became part of village folklore. For years, whenever anyone in the region brought up Rose and the bees, you knew they were talking about the bond of love between mother and child.

Mom spent that entire night in my room, applying tea bags to my stings, holding my hand, and gently singing old Rwandan lullabies to bring me sleep. My mother showed her devotion to me in a thousand ways during her life—but the vision of her coming to me over the rocks would never leave me, nor would it fail to fill my heart with happiness and my eyes with tears. I prayed that if I was ever blessed with a daughter, I'd love her half as much as my mom loved me.

WHEN I OPENED MY EYES, THE BEES WERE GONE. I looked around the room again but couldn't see a single place where they could have entered. It didn't worry me a bit; the more miracles I witnessed, the more willing I was to believe in them.

I felt so comforted and at peace now that I knew my mother was still with me. Her life had been ended by hatred, her body was gone from this world, but her love had transcended death and would never be taken from me. Her spirit was always close by and would reach me whenever I called.

I sensed that she'd come to teach me that living on Earth will always be a battle, that because people are imperfect, we're bound to hurt and disappoint even those we love; in turn, we must accept that we'll be hurt and disappointed, too. My mother knew I needed to learn that lesson and found a way to communicate with me. She knew that I'd recognize her love in the form of bees.

Bryan came by that evening to apologize, but the argument was no longer upsetting me. For the next week, I felt my mother's presence; and when I was alone, I'd talk to her as freely as though she were sitting in the room with me. I told her about everything that was going on in my life—about my work, about the people who had been kind to me and those who had been cruel, and all about the wonderful man I was involved with.

"Seeing" Mom affected me profoundly; I was determined not to rely on others but rather let the Lord provide in all things. So, when I later accepted Bryan's proposal of marriage, it was God I asked to help me plan the wedding.

A traditional Rwandan wedding is a long, complicated, and beautiful event. It has five stages, beginning with the bride-to-be's extended family meeting and evaluating the worthiness of the bridegroom and his family and friends. There is also a lot of negotiation over the dowry between the two families, which usually ends with the groom delivering a cow—the most cherished possession in Rwandan culture—to the bride on the wedding day.

The bride is then escorted to the ceremony by a large entourage sworn to protect her from any dangers she may face along the way. The wedding itself is a richly textured celebration that blends declarations of love for the bride; promises from the groom; an exchange of gifts; and, of course, singing, dancing, music, and food. And one of the great highlights of the ceremony is the presentation of the carefully groomed and decorated cow to the bride, a symbol that she will never want for life's essentials: milk, butter, and manure (used to fertilize the fields).

A traditional wedding is all about family, but because most of my family members were dead, my wedding would be in honor of their memory. My dad, in particular, would have loved a big traditional ceremony. As it is customary for the bride's family to host her wedding, he would have happily done so. In fact, he had that in mind when he built our house by Lake Kivu.

"I chose this land for our home due to the size of the yard and the view of the lake," he'd often tell me when we sat outside to watch the sunset. "We could fit 500 people back here with no problem. You never know when we might have to host a big wedding for someone. And don't you think the lake would be the perfect backdrop for the photos?" Dad would ask me with a wink. It was our little joke. Although he never said that he hoped the wedding would be mine, we both knew that's exactly what he meant.

Because custom demanded that the bride's family pay for the wedding, I was determined to raise the money myself. Bryan would have offered to cover all the costs, but this was going to be my wedding present to my father. He would have been devastated if the groom had broken tradition by footing the bill.

However, money was a problem. At least 200 people could be counted on to show up at a traditional wedding, and that meant I'd need at least one million Rwandan francs. In U.S. currency, that was more than $2,500—almost a year's salary! It was an impossible sum. Kigali was such an expensive place to live, and I had so many other people relying on my monthly paycheck that I had very little money put away. There was only one place where I could go for such a sizable loan.

Dear God, I prayed, *You say in the Bible that no father would give a child a stone if that child asked for bread . . . and for us to imagine what greater gift our Heavenly Father would give us if only we would ask. Well, I have a very big gift to ask for this time: I need money to pay for my wedding. I've never seen that much money before, so I leave it up to You, God. Thank You in advance.*

Bryan and I had set a date, and I'd already invited more than 300 people personally. Unfortunately, with two months to go, I had yet to send out invitations because I hadn't raised any money or found anyone to host the ceremony. For weeks I'd been knocking on doors of distant relatives, asking if they'd allow me to use their backyards for the festivities. But on three separate occasions, I'd been refused—either because the families were too embarrassed by their circumstances to open their homes to guests or because they'd lost too many of their own children during the genocide to open their hearts for a celebration.

With seven weeks left before the wedding, I walked to the home of Dieudonne, who'd been such a good family friend that my brothers and I had called him "uncle" when we were young. I hadn't seen him for many years, but I knew that my parents had helped him buy a house. He remembered me as soon as he opened the door and happily invited me inside.

"It's wonderful to see you again, Immaculée," he said. "I didn't know you were in Kigali; if I had, I would have invited you here long ago. Your parents were so good to me when I was young that I would love to repay their kindness."

I was heartened; Dieudonne had a small place, but a good-sized yard, which was all I needed for the wedding. "Actually, there *is* something you could do to help me," I told him. "I'm getting married, and I need someone to host our wedding. It wouldn't cost you anything, as I'll pay all the expenses . . . but I do need someone to open their home to me."

"I'm sorry, Immaculée. You ask for something I can't give you. Please forgive me, but I will not do this for you." He offered no other reason, but I knew he was worried about money and being embarrassed as a poor host. I would have assured him again that money would be no problem, but I was too crestfallen to argue or plead anymore. It was difficult for me to ask for favors, and receiving four rejections by relatives—no matter how distant—on such a personal and important matter was humiliating. Now I'd run out of relations, since Dieudonne had been my last hope.

By the time I got home to Sarah's, I had a blinding headache, so I went to bed without talking to anyone. There was a letter waiting for me on my pillow from my aunts, Esperance and Jeanne. They were going to fill in for my parents at the wedding, but they now said that they wouldn't make it at all because Interahamwe raiders from Zaire were crossing over into their area every day, killing and terrorizing Tutsis. They wrote:

> *Dear Immaculée,*
> *We're sorry, but there are too many bandits and killers on the road these days for us to travel—five Tutsi women on their way to Kigali were pulled out of a bus and shot dead last week. Please have a nice wedding.*
> *Love,*
> *Jeanne and Esperance*

I crumpled up the letter and collapsed on the mattress. I was asleep within minutes and dreaming about my old home in Mataba. My entire family was there in our backyard, sitting at a picnic table. My mother had prepared all of our favorite courses and had placed them on our finest dishes, on top of our best linen tablecloth. My three brothers were eating ravenously, and my parents sat at the end of the table, holding hands and looking up at me. Behind them, Lake Kivu was shimmering beneath a dusty-rose sunset.

"Isn't that a beautiful view, Immaculée? Perfect for wedding pictures," my father said wistfully.

"Dad, why can't you be at my wedding? No one will have me . . . can't you come back for me?"

"Don't worry, sweetheart. I'll be at your wedding—we will all be. Have faith."

THE NEXT MORNING MY HEADACHE WAS GONE, and I was happy to have seen my family all together again, even if only in a dream. Before I left for work, I picked up the rosary Sarah's mom had given me. All the way to the office, I silently prayed to the Virgin Mary: *Please, Mother, intercede on my behalf as you have so often before. I have asked for such a large favor, and I need all the help I can get. I have invited so many people to a wedding I can't afford, but I know you'll help me, as you always have. Blessed are you among women. Please help your loving daughter.*

After passing through the security gate at the UNDP, I cut across the parking lot, where I noticed a tall, voluptuous African woman wearing an expensive suit sliding out from behind the steering wheel of a new car. It was so unusual to see a woman driving a vehicle in Rwanda that I assumed she must have a rich husband, be a politician, or both. She caught me staring at her, and I thought she was about to scold me for being rude. Instead, she smiled warmly and lifted her right hand toward me. I saw that she was holding a rosary, just as I was.

"You're Immaculée, aren't you?" she called out. "I've been told you love the Virgin Mary almost as much as I do." She made her way over to me and added, "I saw your lips saying a Hail Mary as you passed through the gate, and I knew right away that you're the one they call 'the girl who prays a lot.'"

"It used to be 'the girl who cries a lot,'" I admitted with a laugh.

"Well, we'll have to make sure you don't start crying again, won't we?" She laughed right back and introduced herself as Chantal Kagaba, a Tutsi who had recently started working at the UNDP.

"Did you know that we're sisters?" she asked.

"We are?"

"If the Virgin Mary is my mother and your mother, that makes us sisters, doesn't it?" she explained, slipping her arm though mine. Such familiarity between Rwandan women who just met was unheard of, but I already felt like I'd known Chantal for years. For some reason—perhaps it was her rosary and warm smile, combined with her love of the Blessed Mother—I trusted her right away.

"And as you know, sisters take care of each other, so I'm going to take care of you. You're coming to lunch with me today, Immac-ulée. It's my treat, so don't even try to argue."

"I'd love to have lunch with you, Chantal, but I can pay for myself. You don't have to worry about that."

"You're the one who doesn't have to worry," she replied, as we entered the office.

At noon, my new friend and I drove downtown in her car. I found out that she'd been out of the country during the genocide, but her husband had been killed. Like me, she found solace in prayer to God, the Virgin Mary, and Jesus, or what she called "the Big Three."

"Norah told me that you're getting married," Chantal shared. Norah had been my boss for more than a year. She was a sweet, smart woman from the Netherlands who had become a close friend.

"Yes, in seven weeks." I was nervous to invite someone I barely knew to the ceremony because I still had no money, no food, and no one to host it. But I knew that God and all my saints and guardian angels were working to make it happen, so I asked her to come.

"Of course I will—I wouldn't miss my sister's wedding! I remember my own so well. There were so many people, and the music and the dancers . . . it was so elaborate, so beautiful . . . so damn expensive! My poor father nearly went broke." After parking the car, she confided, "I know your parents are gone, and I know there is no way you could possibly afford a full wedding. So I'd like to help you."

"No! You don't even know me, I couldn't—"

"Don't know me!" Chantal broke in. "I told you, Mary's our mom, so we're sisters! And I don't want to hear one word of argument. My husband left me the house and some money, and I have a good paycheck, so I'm going to help you. That's all there is to it. Now let's get out of the car because we're here."

She was so insistent that I didn't know how to react. I looked out the window and remarked, "But there aren't any restaurants around here."

"I told you I was taking you to lunch, but I didn't say we were going to eat. We're going shopping," she said, pointing to the shop across the street. The sign read, Chez Jojo.

"Jojo's!" I shouted.

"Where else would you get your wedding dress?"

I didn't know what to say. With tears in my eyes, I looked at Chantal and then at the little picture of the Virgin Mary she had taped to her dashboard. "Thank you," I murmured. "Thank you to you both."

"You're welcome. Now let's hurry before our lunch hour is over."

Jojo Nzabamwita had the finest traditional Rwandan bridal gowns and accessories in Rwanda. "Good to see you again," she greeted Chantal as we came in. "So this is the lucky girl you called me about . . . she'll be a gorgeous bride no matter what dress you choose. Pick out whatever you want. Just remember, it may all be imported, but it's still all Rwandan."

Because all the tailors in Kigali had been killed in the genocide, every dress in the shop had come from Uganda or Burundi.

Nevertheless, everything on display was made in the Rwandan style and was beautiful. Chantal and I picked out an elegant dress, the traditional beaded crown worn by the bride, and shoes. It all cost a fortune, but my new friend had already arranged payment with Jojo before we arrived so I wouldn't be embarrassed at the cash register.

"You're an angel, Chantal," I told her as we left Chez Jojo.

"No, but I'm working on it," she said with a grin.

As soon as I got back to work, Norah called me into her office.

"I'm sorry I'm late, Norah," I began.

"Don't be ridiculous," she responded, in the bright Dutch accent that always made her sound happy no matter what her mood. She looked at my shopping bags, smiled, and continued, "I see you've been out with Chantal, which is good. Now it's time for my present. I know that in your culture, the bride's family takes care of the food, and since you're like family to me, Immaculée, I've taken care of it. Everything is going to be catered, and you won't have to think about it at all."

I was so moved I could hardly find the words to thank her. I hugged her tightly and let God and the Blessed Mother know how grateful I was that my prayers were being answered.

And the miracles just kept on coming. As soon as I sat down at my desk, the phone rang. It was my friend Agathe, who'd agreed to be a bridesmaid with my work colleague Claudine.

"Claudine and I have decided that it's too much for you to pay for the bridesmaid dresses for everyone, so we've already bought them. Bye-bye!" she giggled, and hung up.

A couple of hours later, Claudine herself showed up in my office with Chantal, and they were both carrying big paper bags. Without my knowledge, they'd gone through the entire UNDP building asking for donations for the "UN Orphan Bride Fund." They proceeded to empty the bags onto my desk, covering it in a pile of cash two feet deep. There was enough money to pay for the entire wedding without my having to borrow or spend any of my own meager savings. My heart was so full of love for everyone that I thought it would explode.

The phone kept ringing all day. One call was from a co-worker who said that she didn't have any cash to donate but would bring champagne for everyone at the wedding. Another colleague offered her best dining-room chairs so that the bride and groom would be comfortable. The head of the UNDP called to say that he'd make UN vehicles available to me to transport whatever I needed on my special day; he'd also have carpenters build outdoor seating for the guests as soon as I knew where the ceremony was to be held. And people I'd never met dropped by my desk to offer me whatever help they could provide.

I was overwhelmed with kindness and truly basking in the love and power of the Lord. *How deeply You love Your children, God!* my heart sang. *What a beautiful Father you are!*

Then, as I was leaving work, I ran into Sayinzoga, one of my dad's dearest old friends, as well as my mom's distant relative. He'd been a UN volunteer in Senegal for many years and had only recently returned to Rwanda. While we'd passed each other in the halls several times in the past couple of weeks, we'd always been too busy to chat.

"Hello, daughter," he said to me now.

"Sayinzoga, it's nice to see you. My father spoke so fondly of you."

"Leonard was a good man, Immaculée. He was very kind to my family and a wonderful friend to me. And I can see he was an excellent father to you; he raised you well."

"Thank you."

"However, I'm surprised that I must hear certain things about you that you should have told me yourself."

"What things?" I asked, alarmed.

"That you're getting married! I wondered why you haven't asked me to stand in for Leonard. I have a house with a very big yard, and I'd be honored to host your wedding."

"Oh, Sayinzoga! How can I ever thank you?"

"Thank your father. The goodness we do lives after us, and a kindness is never forgotten."

The wedding was the most beautiful I've ever been to—not because it was mine, but because I knew Who had made it happen.

CHAPTER 15

TIME TO LEAVE

The first death threat came after I forgave a murderer.

Being a genocide survivor was dangerous in Rwanda. Thousands of killers continued to live freely in villages across the country, and each one knew that all it would take to send them to prison—or condemn them to death—was for a survivor to accuse them of participating in the slaughter.

Tutsi witnesses, and potential witnesses, disappeared all the time. Others were found dead on lonely stretches of road, floating in rivers and lakes, or even in their beds. Survivors who went to the authorities to report neighbors they personally witnessed killing, torturing, and raping Tutsis became targets of ridicule, mockery, and violence. After my aunts were summoned to court to give testimony against one of their former neighbors, for instance, they were badgered and insulted whenever they left their house. The day after one court appearance, Esperance was attacked in front of her home, thrown to the ground, and kicked half to death. She spent months recovering from the assault.

When I went to the prison near my village to forgive Felicien, the man who'd assisted in the murders of my mother and Damascene, I became a target of the killers as well.

Felicien already stood accused of his crimes against my family. Although I'd recognized his voice while I was hiding in the pastor's house—heard him shouting out that he wanted to find me so I'd become the 400th Tutsi "cockroach" he killed—I had no desire for vengeance. I came to the prison to do only what my heart and my God demanded of me: offer him my forgiveness. And that's exactly what I did. But some Hutu villagers kept a constant eye on the jail to monitor all the comings and goings, and it was assumed that I'd traveled from Kigali to give evidence against Felicien.

A few days later, I visited my aunts, and Jeanne warned, "I'm afraid it's no longer safe for you to come home to see us. We've heard them talking; people think you're testifying. They say you spent three months hiding at Pastor Murinzi's listening to them talk—they think you recognized all of their voices and will identify them to the police. They said it would be better if you were dead, Immaculée! Be careful . . . look what they did to Esperance!"

I was incensed. "Mataba is where I grew up, and it's where my mother and brother are buried. These people took my family from me, Jeanne, and I'm not going to let them drive me from my home."

But things got worse after a reporter from the government newspaper, *Imvaho,* dropped by my office at the UN and started chatting with me. After some small talk, he said, almost as an afterthought, "I was talking to some people in the office about Tutsis who survived the genocide and was told that you had a pretty remarkable story. Is it true that you forgave the man who killed your mom?"

He seemed so friendly that I told him my entire story: about my parents helping people when the killing started; how Pastor Murinzi hid us and lied to the Interahamwe, who suspected we were in his house; the things I had heard the killers say while they hunted for us; and how I discovered God's love and was able to forgive Felicien and the other murderers. The man was so pleasant, and I was so naïve, that I didn't have a clue I'd just been interviewed by a journalist.

The next week the story was published in *Imvaho,* which was circulated all over Rwanda and in neighboring countries as well.

Thousands of people saw it, and those who couldn't read had it read to them. I was traveling to Mataba when the paper came out and didn't know about it until I arrived at Pastor Murinzi's house for a visit.

"What is this, Immaculée?" he demanded, waving a copy of *Imvaho* at me when I knocked on his door. His anger shocked and hurt me. I was always very emotional when I was near the pastor's house, and I wasn't prepared to be attacked by the man who had been my savior.

"How have I offended you, Pastor? I don't know what you're talking about."

"How can you not know?" he asked incredulously, opening the paper to my story and holding it under my nose. "You gave an interview to the government paper, and now the whole country knows what happened here. This is bad, Immaculée—very, very bad."

As my eyes scanned the article, I saw that my words were quoted exactly as I'd spoken them. I was a little upset that I hadn't been clearly informed the interview would be published, but there was nothing wrong with the story, so I didn't see why the pastor was so upset. "I'm sorry," I told him. "I knew that the man was a reporter, but it was a private conversation. Anyway, why does it matter? It's all the truth; there's no harm done."

"No harm? Everybody knows I lied to the Interahamwe now . . . everyone knows that I hid all you Tutsi women."

"You should be proud of what you did, Pastor. You saved our lives, and you did what God wanted you to do. This is such a good example of the kind of love people should have for each other, and it shows Tutsis that there are brave Hutus who risked their lives to help during the genocide."

"How can you live through so much and stay so foolish, Immaculée? This story makes me look like a traitor to the Hutus. Do you know how many Interahamwe there are around here? Now they're going to think that I told you about Felicien and what he said. People are killed for less than that every day. You should be concerned about keeping quiet and being invisible, not blabbing about what happened in my house. *Never* talk about what happened here."

"How can you say that?!" I cried. "You want me to keep secrets about someone who killed my parents? Do you want me to betray my parents the way I betrayed Vianney when you made me tell him to leave this house . . . when you made me send him to his death?" Hot tears were shooting from my eyes as I thought about my first night in hiding, especially since I was standing in the very spot where I'd last seen my brother alive.

"Do you expect me to hide from the men who murdered my family?" I went on. "They're dead, and they deserve justice. I will forgive their killers, but I will not hide from them—and I will not lie for them. You and I are alive, Pastor, and we know the truth— we have to speak out! We have to speak for the dead because no one else is left to tell their story!"

Pastor Murinzi sighed wearily. "Do what you want with yourself; I have enough troubles of my own to worry about you. But please, do me a favor to repay me for saving your life: Forget about me, and forget about my house. Forget that I ever hid you, Immaculée. Good-bye."

The pastor closed the door, and I walked through his garden feeling like a child who'd been unjustly whipped by a parent. I loved the pastor for his kindness during the genocide, but I was so furious with him for trying to cover up what had happened. I was also angry at the way he'd spoken to me; if my parents were alive, he would have shown me more respect.

I knew that many Hutus who hadn't participated in the genocide, or those who had helped Tutsis, didn't want to talk about what had happened. They wanted to keep what they'd done secret from their families because it was their brothers and fathers and sons who had done the killing. Still, it weighed on me that Pastor Murinzi and I had had a falling-out.

After the genocide, I had a recurring nightmare that I was running through the village in the middle of the night, hunted by killers and snarling dogs that snapped at my feet. Every house I passed was dark and locked except for the pastor's, which was lit up like a beacon. In my dream, he was always standing in the doorway, waiting for me to get safely inside before he closed the door against the killers. Now, after our argument, I wouldn't be able go near his house without thinking of our broken friendship and that I was no longer welcome in his home.

Thankfully, this tale would have a happy ending. It took many years, but God eventually brought the pastor and me back together. We became friends again and proudly shared our story with others.

THE NEWSPAPER ARTICLE THAT HAD PUSHED PASTOR MURINZI AND ME apart also brought me a lot of dangerous attention. Thousands of killers had passed through our village during the genocide, and now they all had reason to worry that I'd overheard them making plans to kill—or worse, that I'd actually heard them killing people on the road in front of the pastor's house. My life was in the hands of God, so I didn't spend too much time worrying about how many individuals might want me dead. But as time passed and more arrests were made, I was aware of how exposed to danger I was, especially when I traveled home to visit my mother's grave.

By the summer of 1996, the Interahamwe killers and ex-Hutu soldiers running the refugee camps in Zaire were staging major attacks on border communities such as Mataba. More and more Tutsis were being killed, and horror stories about the Interahamwe raping and exploiting Hutu refugees in our neighboring country were spreading everywhere.

Paul Kagame—who was vice president of Rwanda at this point, but its true military and political leader—went on the radio every week assuring innocent Hutu refugees that they could come home without fear of death or imprisonment. At the same time, he would plead for help from the international community to stop the Interahamwe from committing atrocities in Zaire and murdering Tutsis in Rwanda. "Save our people from these killers in the jungle or we will do it ourselves," Kagame simultaneously begged and warned the West and United Nations.

Despite repeated requests for an international force to clear the Interahamwe from Zairian camps and free the Hutu refugees, no one outside Rwanda would get involved in the conflict. Finally, in late 1996, Kagame sent his troops into Zaire and attacked the Interahamwe himself.

There was terrible fighting in the jungle, but when the Interahamwe retreated from Kagame's forces, hundreds of thousands of Hutu refugees escaped from the hellish camps and flooded back into Rwanda. I watched the news reports flickering across the UN's television sets with disbelief. The entire Hutu exodus that had left our nation three years before seemed to be returning in an enormous surge. A line of refugees 180 miles long twisted across Zaire toward the Rwandan border, and so many of them were emaciated, sick, and ragged. The sides of the road were strewn with the bodies of the old and very young who'd simply dropped dead from the exertion. The view from my office window was disturbing as well, as the streets of Kigali were filling with Hutu refugees.

There were problems with the rush of returnees; for Tutsis, the biggest concern was that so many Hutus had crossed the border so quickly that it was impossible to know how many killers were hiding in their midst. How many had weapons hidden beneath their rags? How many were Interahamwe, or had been recruited and trained to launch another genocide? No one knew, but everyone worried.

A few weeks after the horde of refugees spilled out of Zaire, the Tanzanian government closed down the Hutu refugee camps in its country. Another half-million homeless Hutus returned to Rwanda from different directions, and this time the influx was even faster. The number of Hutu refugees coming into Rwanda in those few short weeks nearly equaled the size of the entire Tutsi population! The question was: Would they settle peacefully, or would there be a new revolution and another bloody conflict?

BRYAN WANTED ME TO STOP WALKING TO WORK because he felt that the streets had become too dangerous. I didn't want to feel like a prisoner in my own country again, so I kept on walking. But four years after the genocide, it seemed as if everyone who lived in Rwanda was in fact being held prisoner.

The trials for the organizers of the holocaust were starting in Arusha, Tanzania; and the trials of "ordinary" Hutu killers were gearing up in our own city of Kigali. More than 100,000 Hutus were in jail waiting to face their accusers, and more than 1,000 suspected killers were being arrested every month. But the scales of justice were askew: Thousands of Hutus who had committed crimes were never arrested, but thousands who were arrested—while likely guilty—were locked up without charges ever being filed against them. And then there were many totally innocent Hutus falsely accused of crimes by former Tutsi friends or neighbors hungry for revenge. John's brother Christian became one of these victims of Tutsi vengeance by false accusation, an act of injustice I could not stand by and watch.

Christian's best friend, Sammy, was a Tutsi. They'd been lifelong pals, playing on the same soccer team as teenagers and going off to university together. Their ethnic differences had never affected their friendship, and Christian also spoke out against extremism and advocated equal rights for all tribes. During much of the genocide, Christian had stayed at Pastor Murinizi's, who was his uncle. From the bathroom, I often overheard him talking outside, and he was one of the few Hutus I ever heard speak out openly against what was being done to the Tutsis.

Sammy joined the Tutsi rebel army to fight against the extremist Hutus and Interahamwe. When he returned from the war, he found the bodies of his parents and siblings on the floor of his childhood home. Then Sammy went to Christian's and saw his old pal and his family living together in the big house they'd grown up in. Sammy began to resent Christian, and his resentment grew into hatred.

While the rest of Christian's family moved to Zambia, Christian stayed behind in Rwanda. A friend of mine who worked with him told me that Sammy showed up at their office one day and pulled a gun on Christian. Sammy started shouting, "This man is a killer! He killed every day during the genocide! I'm taking him to prison; don't anyone try to stop me." And no one did.

At Kigali Central Prison, Sammy turned Christian over to the jailor and said that he'd witnessed Christian murder his family.

Christian protested, but Sammy had fought for the rebels, and his word carried a lot of weight. Christian was locked up with the general population.

The prison was a dark fortress that I went out of my way to avoid. Whenever I passed within earshot of the enormous redbrick monstrosity—which looked like a blood-drenched tombstone jutting out of Avenue de la Justice—I always heard screaming. Nearly 8,000 Hutu prisoners had been crammed behind the ugly walls in a space designed for a quarter of that number. There were old men and boys as young as 11 or 12 living in the same filthy quarters, forced to fight for food and defend themselves from jailhouse thieves, thugs, and sexual predators.

I couldn't let Christian rot in that dark hole and wait for a trial that might never come. I'd lived through a horrible injustice and seen my family fall victim to it—if the new Rwanda was to be a just and godly nation, we had to do what was right. Besides the fact that I knew where Christian was during the genocide, I also knew he could never commit murder, for he was one of the gentlest souls I'd ever met. So, as loathsome and frightening a place as that prison was to me, I had to go there to speak on Christian's behalf.

Even in the segregated section I was escorted through, the air smelled like death; my stomach started to turn the moment I stepped into the jail through the heavy iron door. Then, through a small window cut into the brick, I caught a glimpse of the main courtyard, where thousands of emaciated men wearing filthy pink shirts milled about, pressed so tightly against each other that there was no room for them to move more than a foot or two at a time. I shuddered as I thought about what it must be like to live under such conditions, facing a lifetime of imprisonment with only persecution, pain, and guilt to look forward to. How much worse it must be to be trapped here, knowing you were falsely accused, an innocent man in a sea of monsters.

God, please send some angels to this dungeon, I immediately asked Him. *These poor souls are buried so deep in darkness that they may never find You on their own.*

"What are you doing here asking to see a Hutu killer?" inquired the jailor I was brought to see.

"You have an innocent man locked up here," I replied.

He laughed. "Would you like to point him out to me?" he asked, waving his hand toward the main courtyard. "I have 8,000 'innocent' killers in my jail."

"His name is Christian, and he's a friend of mine. He was turned in by a man named Sammy, who told lies about him. I have proof that he's innocent, and I'm not going to leave until you tell me that you're going to set him free."

The jailor shook his head and went through his "records," which consisted of an assortment of torn and crumpled pieces of paper held together with a bit of twine. There was no arrest record for Christian, but, remarkably, the man did find my friend's name scribbled on one of the pages he was holding.

"I actually remember this guy," the jailor told me. "I can't give you any promises, but I'll look into it. Now, don't ever come back here again. People will think you're either a traitor or a witness, and it will cause you trouble. No good will come to you from this place."

I never did go back to the horrible prison, but some good *did* come from my visit: Christian was freed by the end of that day. He later married a foreign-aid worker from Europe and moved to Switzerland to raise a family.

However, the jailor was right about the prison bringing me trouble. A short while afterward, my name was published in Rwanda's other big newspaper—I was identified as a genocide survivor, an eyewitness to murder, and a resident of Kigali.

"Time to leave," Bryan said after seeing the paper.

The next day, a Hutu friend of mine from the UN gave me this stark warning: "You know I didn't have anything to do with the killing, Immaculée, but some people I know did, and I heard them mentioning your name last night. I don't know what they were talking about, but it has something to do with Tutsis testifying at the trials. You should be careful."

If that wasn't enough to worry me, I received word that my cousin Agnus, a nun who lived in the north, had been pulled off a bus with 30 other Tutsis by Interahamwe insurgents, stripped naked, and shot. All of the other passengers were killed, but Agnus survived because she had so much of the other victims' blood on her that the killers assumed she was dead.

That week there was terrible news all over Rwanda about major Interahamwe raids where dozens of Tutsis were murdered, many by machete. Our national nightmare appeared to be starting all over again.

Then, in the middle of all of this bad news, I received the best news I'd ever had in my life: I was pregnant. In the midst of more death, I had life within me.

I placed my hands on my gently swelling belly and thanked God for the greatest of all the gifts He had given me. I'd been blessed with a new life, which I had to protect. Bryan was right—it was time to leave my homeland.

CHAPTER 16

IN AMERICA

We dipped through the clouds, and I was there, floating above a new world of glass and steel and buildings so tall they touched the sky. New York City revealed itself to me: I could see the harbor below and the torch of the Statue of Liberty pointing toward my future. The late-afternoon sun shimmered across a million windows, and the city looked as if it were carved from gold. When I was a little girl in Mataba, I never dreamed that such a place could exist. An endless array of towers jutted skyward from Manhattan like a concrete mountain range soaring above deep canyons filled with cars and people—more people than in all of Rwanda! I placed my hand on my belly and waited for the telltale kick that let me know my baby was with me and doing well.

Look at all those busy people down there, little one, I mused, as the plane descended toward the airport. *We don't have to worry about being lonely in our new life.*

Bryan and I moved into a house in a suburb called Rosedale, in the borough of Queens, which was about as different from Rwanda as I could imagine. The neighborhood was nice enough—a mixture of many races with a strong core of recent Caribbean immigrants—but I didn't really get to know anyone. Family houses lined the streets, but they were set back from the road and sidewalks by big front yards concealed behind bushes and fences. Residents also tended to dart into their homes from their cars without paying much attention to their neighbors.

Back in Mataba, people lived with their doors open and knew each other . . . and if they didn't, they got acquainted quickly. Newcomers could expect visitors bearing gifts for many days, so they wouldn't remain strangers for long. The village welcomed new people warmly and made them feel at home. Even when Kigali was recovering from the chaos after the genocide, there was a sense of community; no matter where I went in the city, someone I knew was sure to greet me. But I arrived in Rosedale without knowing a soul, and the community wasn't the easiest place for newcomers to make friends or even meet their neighbors.

My husband had arranged for a job transfer to the UN's world headquarters in Manhattan. When we arrived from Rwanda in August 1998, he took a month's leave of absence so that we could get organized in the house; but by September, he was back on his full-time schedule, leaving for work early in the morning and returning late in the evening. Traffic, I would learn, played a determining role in the amount of time people spent with each other in New York. My mother-in-law, Eileen, lived with us for a while, but she had a job caring for the elderly and was gone most of the day, too.

So, after all the excitement of moving to America, I settled into a life as a suburban housewife and expectant mother. It wasn't exactly what I'd envisioned when I boarded the plane in Kigali, but I had a home and what mattered most: my unborn baby was safe from harm. To pass the time, I taught myself how to cook Trinidadian dishes for Bryan using his mother's recipe book.

The first weeks of my new life in the United States were also spent trying to grasp the subtleties of American culture, for which my previous exposure had been pretty much limited to whatever French-dubbed U.S. films the nuns played for us at my Catholic high school. The two I particularly remembered were *Rambo* with Sylvester Stallone, and *Coming to America* with Eddie Murphy—but neither film prepared me for real life in the United States, where people shopped in a place called Costco that was bigger than Kigali International Airport. When I saw the abundance of goods Americans had to choose from, I understood why so much space was necessary.

The endless rows of long aisles looked exactly alike, except for the different products on the shelves, and I got lost in the maze of consumer goods. The amount of food was almost frightening: I'd never before seen a can of beans large enough to feed an entire Rwandan family for a week. And it wasn't just food—if people wanted, they could buy a TV in one aisle, find pounds of fresh fish in the next, choose an entire new wardrobe in another, and pick up a set of car tires on their way to the checkout. There was such bounty, but nobody else seemed to notice; that is, except for my neighbor Smith, and he hadn't made a purchase in years.

Smith was the first friend I made in America, and for many months, he was my only friend. We met on the day I attempted to make my first *pelau,* a Trinidadian chicken-and-rice dish. I'd been unhappy with the outcome of my meal and was tossing it in the trash when I saw Smith doing yard work next door. He didn't make the greatest first impression: He was wearing jeans and a white T-shirt that was so dirty it had become dark gray, and his pants were stained with grease and ragged at the bottom. As we'd say in Rwanda, it looked like the cow had chewed his clothes and spit them out. But then I noticed the humble way he looked at me and the kind and sincere smile that lit up his face. I saw that he had a good heart and knew that we'd become friends.

"Hi, I'm Smith," he said, and came over to shake my hand. "Welcome to the neighborhood."

"Hello, Smith. My name is Immaculée."

"Where are you from?"

"Rwanda."

"Ah, you're from Africa. You speak English and African! I love your president, Nelson Mandela."

I laughed. The few people I'd met in New York so far all seemed to think Africa was one big country with one leader. "Africa is a continent with more than 50 countries, Smith," I corrected him. "There's not one African language; there are about 2,000 different languages."

"Wow, you must have to remember an awful lot of words," he replied with a chuckle. "But I still like your president. Mandela is my hero!" Smith looked through the open door of our house and sniffed appreciatively. "Your home doesn't smell African . . . it smells Trinidadian . . . it smells good!"

"My husband is Trinidadian. I'm learning to cook his food, but I'm not very good yet."

"Well, that smells like a perfectly cooked pelau, and I should know—I'm Trinidadian, and pelau is my favorite dish," my neighbor encouraged me. He gave me a sweet smile and then returned to his chores.

When I mentioned meeting Smith to Bryan that night, he told me that he had already met him and had hired him to do some work in our basement. Bryan also thought that he was a good fellow and trustworthy, so the next time I saw Smith, I invited him in to sample my latest attempt at Trinidadian cuisine.

"Oh my," he said with a full mouth. "Are you sure you're from Africa? This pelau tastes like you grew up in Trinidad."

Smith was wearing different clothes from when I first met him, but these were just as rumpled and soiled as the others had been. As we got to know each other, he explained his circumstances. He told me that he'd grown up in Trinidad in a house near the ocean, with loving parents and three brothers who'd been inseparable. His early memories were very happy ones, but when he was six years old, his mother became ill and died. "After Mom passed away, my dad got drunk and stayed that way. The government put my brothers and me in different foster homes, and I never saw them again. A few years later, I heard that my father died from drinking, and that's the story of how I became an orphan.

"I made a new life in America. I had a good job as a plumber, and I married a woman I loved. We had a house and a child, and we were happy . . . but my child got older and moved far away. Then my wife's rich aunt died, and she left me so that she wouldn't have to share the inheritance. After she left, nothing mattered to me anymore. Things were very hard for a long time. My mother hadn't lived long enough to teach me how to clean or cook or wash the clothes, and when my wife left, I couldn't be bothered to learn."

After a moment, he continued, "I don't care how I look, and I don't care what I have. Everybody else thinks things are what make us happy, but being a good person, like God wants us to be, *that* is what's important. People in this country truly believe that they can buy happiness, which is why the stores are so big; they think that bigger things mean bigger happiness. The only thing I have is myself and God, and I'm happy."

Smith came by the house often to chat. As many of my friends had done in Rwanda, he warned me that I was too trusting of people. "You're African, Immaculée, so you need to be careful," he cautioned "You can't be as nice to everyone as you are to me. People will treat you poorly because you're black."

"Why would anyone do that to me?"

"Don't you know what's going on in this country? Haven't you heard about prejudice against blacks?"

"You mean slavery? I know about that, but it ended a long time ago, Smith. You don't mean that it's still going on?"

"You've got a lot to learn, Immaculée. Sometimes blacks are discriminated against simply for being black. It is an evil thing, but it's a fact. There is a lot of hatred here . . . as an African, you'll find yourself a victim of racism."

"Oh no, what you're saying *can't* be true," I protested. "I ran away from a place that had so much hatred and discrimination that people killed their own neighbors and family members— don't tell me there is more of the same in America! I thought that racial hatred was a part of history here . . . the Civil War ended more than a century ago, didn't it?"

"Some things never end," my friend replied sadly. "I'm sorry to upset you by saying these things, but it's better that you know the truth. You can't go around trusting everyone here."

"I'm sorry, Smith, but even if what you say is true, I always have to do my best to love people and give them a chance to love me back. I can't suspect others of evildoing for no reason at all; that's what causes hatred and distrust in the first place."

"Good luck to you, then," Smith said. "But if anyone hurts you, you come to me."

While it was hard for me to believe my friend's troubling comments on race relations in the United States, it somehow made me less uneasy about Rwanda. This all put what had happened between Hutus and Tutsis in a larger perspective, making the hatred seem less personal. Now I saw how the evil bigotry that had led to the genocide plagued all tribes and races in all parts of the world, not just in my country. The same prejudices existed everywhere—between rich and poor, men and women, people of different religions and different colors. And if evil was universal, we could all work together against the common enemy.

RWANDA WAS CALLED "THE LAND OF ETERNAL SPRING" because the weather was so pleasant and comfortable throughout the year. Back home, we never had to worry about heating our houses or knitting thick sweaters or other warm clothing . . . which wasn't true in New York. By late October, chilly winds were ripping the dying leaves from the trees in Rosedale. It was the first time in my life I'd known the cold, and there was nothing about it I enjoyed.

Even though I was now in my eighth month of pregnancy, my morning sickness was worse than ever. I was so big and sore that I couldn't bend over, the smallest household task felt impossible, and even reading could make me violently nauseated. All I could do to pass the time was sit in the living room with a bucket next to me and stare out the window as the relentless north wind whipped any last trace of summer from Queens.

The days dragged painfully by, and the walls of my new home grew smaller by the hour. During one in a long succession of sleepless nights, I gripped my rosary and silently asked the Virgin Mary for help: *You have always come to me in my need, Mother, and I'm going crazy sitting around all night and day waiting to throw up. I know you faced much more serious problems carrying your baby, but please ease my sickness while I wait for my little one to come.*

The next morning, I was staring out the window trying to hold down a cup of tea when I heard distant church bells. Since moving to New York, I hadn't been to church at all because of my morning sickness. But now I pushed myself out of my chair, put aside my bucket, and dressed in every warm shirt and sweater I could get my hands on. I had to find those bells.

The ivory-colored bricks of St. Clare's Parish looked warm and inviting as I waddled toward the main door beneath the lofty bell tower. Inside, the church was beautiful and spacious, with a double row of marble pillars flanking the middle pews, and seven stained-glass windows depicting biblical history running down the length of either wall. Morning Mass was about to begin, and I embraced the ritual like a dear friend who had been away too long.

For the next month, I treated my morning sickness by going to Mass every day. It didn't cure me completely, but it was excellent medicine. When there was no else to talk to, visiting a house of God always alleviated my loneliness and took my mind off of my physical discomfort. In long hours of prayer, I was able to properly thank the Lord for delivering me safely from Rwanda and ask Him for the one gift I now wanted more than anything else: a healthy, happy child.

Later I would kick myself for not using that time at St. Clare's to also pray for a quick and painless delivery.

"MOM!" MY SCREAMS ECHOED THROUGH THE HALLWAYS OF THE HOSPITAL, where I labored for 18 hours. All I could do was cry out to the woman who should have warned me about the agony of childbirth—had she done so, I might have entered a convent like I'd planned when I was a girl.

How did you survive this torture, Mom? You must have loved me more than I ever knew if you suffered like this to give birth to me. Oh God!

The first time Bryan asked me how much it hurt, I ripped the curtains off the wall. Six hours later, when he asked me again, I yanked the bed so hard that the metal bar on the side broke off in my hand. But at the end of it all, on November 13, 1998, my darling Nikeisha was born. She was beautiful, she was healthy . . . but she wasn't very happy. She came into the world crying, and she kept on crying. The doctor assured my husband and me that all was fine; Nikki was just colicky and would settle down in a few days.

But the poor child cried for weeks and weeks. She never slept for more than 30 or 40 minutes at a stretch, and when she awoke she'd pick up her full-volume bawling where she'd left off. I was awake with her the entire time, feeding her with my eyes half open, napping for minutes at a time, changing diapers in my sleep.

Bryan had taken all the time off from his job that he was allowed when we first moved to New York, so he had to be at work. His mother had a lingering cold and had to stay in her room so that the baby wouldn't catch it—although we lived in the same house, it would be a month before she'd be able to hold her beautiful new granddaughter. Therefore, my first months of motherhood were as emotionally and physically draining as the time I'd spent hiding from killers in Pastor Murinzi's bathroom. The pain of missing my parents, especially my mother, came rushing back to me, filling me with new heartache as I helplessly cradled my screaming newborn in my arms.

"Mom, can't you help me . . . can't you help me, please?" I'd mumble under my breath, trying to keep myself awake to feed Nikki whenever she'd stop crying enough to take a little milk.

What made those days even more difficult was imagining the glorious welcome my daughter would have received in Mataba, since the birth of a child is one of the greatest life events for every Rwandan family and village.

During that first week after a baby is born, the mother is ordered to lie down for seven days while her friends and female family members tend to all of her needs and those of the infant. The new mother is forbidden from seeing the sun for a week, thus ensuring that she recuperates fully in bed. On the seventh day, she is dressed in traditional clothing, a crown is placed on her head, and her baby is handed to her so that she can officially begin her role as a mother.

The next day a huge meal is cooked, and all the children in the village are summoned to the mother's hut to eat their fill. The little ones then sit in a circle around the mother, and each child holds the new arrival and suggests a name for him or her. On the ninth day, the father chooses one of the names the village children selected, or he invents one of his own based on what he sees when he first looks into his child's eyes. Finally, a community party is held to welcome the newborn into God's kingdom on Earth.

But in Rosedale, there was no one to sit with me. There was no rest, no naming ceremony, and no celebratory feast. There was only my baby's crying.

A few weeks after Nikki was born, winter began with a frigid blast of arctic air. Two feet of something cold and wet and miserable called "snow" dropped from the sky, burying the city and trapping me in my home. It was so cold that my infant and I couldn't have left the house even if we'd been awake enough, well enough, or brave enough to try. I sat up with her until dawn each morning.

Two months of my daughter's suffering had worn down my heart and exhausted my energy. One subzero January night, I stood cradling her in my arms, looking through the window at snowdrifts piled up against my neighbors' locked doors. The world and everything in it seemed frozen.

Pressing my baby tightly to my bosom, I knelt in the middle of the floor and called out to God: "Lord, I'm sorry, but I can't do this! You have given me this beautiful child, but I'm failing . . . maybe You have made a mistake. I'm not ready to be a mother, and I'm so sorry to have let You down. The doctors say there's nothing wrong with her, but I can't ease her pain or stop her tears. I'm tired and sick and hurting inside. I'm at the end of my rope, and I don't think I can last much longer like this . . . please, God, help me."

Within a few days, my prayer was answered. My sweet little girl slept quietly through an entire night, and when she awoke, her eyes were clear, and the smile on her face has yet to go away. From that night forward, she slept peacefully from the moment I put her down at night until she woke me with her laughter in the morning. The trauma of those early weeks of parenthood slipped into distant memory, replaced by the incomparable joy I found in being a mother.

WHEN NIKKI WAS EIGHT MONTHS OLD, I DECIDED IT WAS TIME for me to go back to work. She was the center of my life, but something was pulling me forward. I believed that God had spared me to share my story with the world, which meant that I had to get myself back in it. Fortunately, I knew where I could reach the world without leaving New York City—the world headquarters of the United Nations was just across the East River in Manhattan. God had helped me get a job at the UN in Kigali when I was a penniless refugee, and I could see no reason why He wouldn't do the same for me now.

Bryan, however, did not share my enthusiasm. "Immaculée, you're an African immigrant who has just arrived in America," he told me. "When people come to this country, they start small and work their way up—that's how things are done. No one is going to hire you at the UN." He thought that if I wanted to work, my aspirations should begin more modestly.

Although Bryan had a good job at the United Nations and could have put in a good word for me, he worried about his good name and reputation as a fair and honest employee, since nepotism was considered to be highly inappropriate. He wanted to help me, but until I could improve my typing skills and my English, he suggested that I get a job cleaning homes or offices.

Sometimes my husband and I didn't see things the same way. There was nothing wrong with working at a cleaning job, but all you had to do was look around our home to see that I wasn't cut out for housework. Besides, I knew God had something else in mind for me, and I didn't want to disappoint Him.

During our next shopping trip to Costco, I bought a speed-typing program for our home computer and spent every night for the next three months practicing my typing as Nikki slept in her crib next to me. In 90 days, I had tripled my speed and doubled my accuracy.

My next step was to find a trustworthy babysitter. I met a lovely Jamaican woman named Gloria who was highly recommended by the priest at St. Clare's, and she agreed to watch Nikki for a day so that I could go into the city and look for a job. I had one contact at the UN—a supervisor from the New York office named Arturo, who'd come to Kigali for a week to see our operation there. I'd spoken with him for only a few moments, but he'd given me his card and told me to drop by his office if I was ever in Manhattan. So I was all set: I had my new typing skills, a job contact, and a babysitter. All that was left was to notify God that it was time to go to work.

For seven days, I bundled my daughter up, hiked over to St. Clare's, and prayed in that beautiful church every morning. I also meditated and fasted to clear my mind and body. And before I went to bed each night, I made sure to forgive all the people who had ever angered or upset me, sending prayers of blessing to all of them. After a week of this, I told Bryan that I'd be joining him on his drive to the office the next day and explained my plan: "All I need you to do is drop me off outside the building at 8 A.M. and pick me up at 6 P.M. when you're leaving for home. I'll do the rest." So, early the next morning, he left me standing on First Avenue and wished me luck.

"What is your business at the UN today, miss?" the guard in the front lobby asked me.

I gave him Arturo's card.

"Is he expecting you?"

"He told me to drop by," I answered honestly, and was directed to the elevator. A few minutes later, Arturo's secretary escorted me into his office, and I was shaking hands with the only professional person in Manhattan whose name I knew.

Arturo was very pleasant at first, offering me a seat and a cup of tea. But when he asked me what I was doing in New York and I replied that I was looking for a job, his demeanor quickly changed. His eyes appraised me in a new light, and it didn't look so good.

All those months locked up in the house with Nikki hadn't done much for my complexion or my figure. I looked drawn from weeks of sleep deprivation and was toting around quite a bit of my pregnancy weight. My hair could have looked better; and my clothes, while the best in my wardrobe, had come with me from Rwanda and were certainly not the latest in New York business attire. In a glance, Arturo had shaken my confidence to the core—instead of a hopeful job candidate, I felt like a frumpy housewife.

"Please excuse me for a moment," he said politely and left his office. It wasn't long before his secretary came in and told me that Arturo had been called away unexpectedly. As she escorted me to the elevator, she added that there weren't any job openings in the office and it would be a waste of time for me to return.

That's it? I thought, as I stood downstairs again. *I've been in the city for ten minutes and I've completely exhausted my job prospects?* There was no one else for me to see, and I couldn't get past security without at least the name of someone who worked there.

As the morning rush of employees swept around me, I took my rosary from my purse and silently prayed in the middle of the busy lobby: *I've done everything I can to be ready for this, Lord. Bryan will be picking me up at 6, so I'm on a tight schedule. Please send me someone who can help me find a job here right away.*

Before I could even finish my prayer, two women walked by me speaking to each other in Kinyarwanda, and I shouted, "Hey, you're Rwandans!"

They were as surprised as I was to hear someone else speaking our language—even in multiethnic Manhattan, Kinyarwanda isn't heard very often. The two of them were delighted to meet another Rwandan, and we were soon chatting like old friends. When I shared what had happened with Arturo, one of the gals laughed and said, "Oh, he's a dog. You wouldn't want to work for him anyway!" Then the other one wrote down the name and number of a supervisor in another department. "Tell her I told you to drop by," she urged, and both women wished me luck.

By the end of the day I was sitting in the office of a lovely French-Canadian woman who was in charge of hiring for the United Nations World Food Programme. She'd traveled to Rwanda and loved our culture—and she'd even stayed at the Christus

Center when she was in Kigali! We talked in her office for two hours about everything from the flavor of the country's notorious banana beer to our faith in God and how much we both believed in the power of prayer.

As people in her office were getting ready to go home, the woman remembered that I'd come to see her about a job. "There really isn't anything available," she told me, "but something tells me you'd fit in here. I can't promise you anything, but if something comes up, you'll be the first one I call."

When Bryan picked me up and asked me how my day went, I gave him a big smile and responded that everything had worked out fine.

I prayed every day for the next two weeks for the phone to ring, and when it did, it was my new French-Canadian friend with news that someone in the office was taking an extended vacation. "It's a three-month contract," she said. "It's not much, but it's a foot in the door. The rest will be up to you, Immaculée."

Up to me and God, I silently corrected her.

Just like so many other blessings in my life, I found that job through prayer. I could see God everywhere in my life: Eight months after leaving Rwanda, I'd been given a new home, a new baby, and an exciting new job in New York City. And before the year was out, I'd take my first steps to fulfill the purpose God had chosen for my life.

CHAPTER 17

THE WORLD HEARS MY STORY

My past flowed through my mind faster than my fingers could type. A torrent of words poured from my heart in a cathartic flood of memory that lasted three months.

The writing frenzy had been triggered by a simple head cold my daughter caught in May 2000. Her crying had awakened me in the middle of the night and started an emotional chain reaction that took 100,000 words to quell. Nikki's suffering made me think about my mother and how I needed her to teach me how to care for my little one. That made me think about how Nikki would have loved her grandmother, which made me think about how much my entire family would have spoiled my baby rotten. And that made me think about how I'd lost everyone in the genocide.

My mind began racing backward toward April 1994. Everything I'd seen and felt and heard, all that I'd touched and smelled and perceived, came welling up through my mind and senses so vividly that I felt as if I were reliving every moment.

I believe that God had talked to me through Nikki's sobs, reminding me that the millions of tears I'd shed myself since the genocide now made up the ink to write my story.

THREE WEEKS AFTER TYPING MY FIRST SENTENCE, the bulk of the manuscript for *Left to Tell* had been completed. But I came back to it again and again over the next four years whenever I thought of something to add, such as a detail of my childhood, a funny story about my brothers, the hunting songs of the killers, or tales of my parents' strength and kindness. And then I'd think of the way God's love enveloped my heart and try to find words to describe a love that defied description. Finally, I knew I was finished, and it was time to turn all the pages I'd typed into a book. Unfortunately, I had no idea if anyone would want to read it or how to get it published.

I picked up the Yellow Pages and began looking for publishing houses in New York City, but I decided that it would be easier and faster to let God do the searching. I placed the manuscript in a box beside my Bible and left the rest up to Him. As usual, I took out my rosary to pray—but in keeping with my new vocation, I decided that I should put my prayer into words as well. I picked up a pen and wrote this letter:

> *Dear Lord,*
> *Thanks for helping me finish the manuscript. I hope it's what You had in mind. But now that it's done, You have to find someone to print it and then put it in the window display at Barnes & Noble. This is really Your story more than mine, and I'm looking forward to reading it once You have made it into a book.*
> *Thank You again, God.*
> *Your loving daughter,*
> *Immaculée*

I put the letter in an envelope, sealed it, and placed it in the middle of the manuscript. Three days later, God introduced me to the man who would get my book published.

Through some of my UN friends, I'd been invited to attend a weekend conference on spirituality, and one of the workshops dealt with facing the fear of death. The instructor told the 200 people in the room to lie on the floor, get comfortable, close their eyes, and imagine the person they'd like to meet when their spirit crossed over to heaven. I immediately pictured my father.

As the workshop leader gently urged us to set our imaginations free, I felt my spirit lift from my body and float upward, through the ceiling, into the dark sky, and toward a brilliant bright light. And there was my dad, waiting for me in a pool of golden sun, looking happier than I'd ever seen him. He spoke to me in a voice that echoed in my mind: *Hello, Immaculée. I'm glad to see you looking so happy and well. Remember, we are always with you; you are never alone. Every prayer you say is heard, and all your prayers will be answered.*

I tried to express how much I missed him, but my mouth couldn't form words. There was no need for words, however, since he knew all I had to say; in return, I could feel all the love he had for me. It was heaven.

Then I heard another voice, instructing, "Slowly come back down . . . let go of what you're seeing, let go of what you're feeling, and come back down."

The workshop leader's voice reached my consciousness from a great distance, beckoning me to leave my father's warm light and return to the floor of the conference room. Everything in my soul rejected her summons; I didn't ever want to leave my father's presence.

Dad! I cried to him, as I was tugged downward. *Dad!* But the light faded, and I felt somebody shaking me. Several people were kneeling at my side, rocking me by my shoulders. "Come out of it, Immaculée!" someone said. "Are you all right?"

My skin was flushed, still warm from the light, and I managed to whisper, "I'm fine, I'm just fine." I would have felt foolish if my heart hadn't been so happy. For a few moments I was giddy with pleasure. I couldn't make out what those gathering around me were saying because I had choirs singing in my mind.

I was with my dad, I thought blissfully, smiling at the faces around me.

"Are you sure you're okay?" the instructor asked. "This exercise can be very intense, and you're not the only one who was slow coming back."

"I feel wonderful, won . . ." Before the word could leave my mouth the second time, however, I suddenly felt wretched. My stomach lurched, my eyes gushed, and I wailed so loudly that all the activity in the room came to a standstill. The afterglow of love that had radiated in me after seeing my father had cooled to the point that I was left with a palpable sense of emptiness.

A few kind souls put their arms around my shoulders and comforted me, and the sorrow vanished as quickly as it had come. I was left with the memory of the smile on my dad's face, as well as his promise that my prayers were being heard. I took a deep breath and headed outside to get some fresh air.

As I walked through the lobby, I noticed a very happy-looking man sitting at a table signing books. He had a warm, open face and such a sincere smile that I was drawn to him immediately. I'd seen him a few times over the course of the weekend, but I didn't know his name. I assumed he was one of the speakers and probably a writer, which explained the signing.

I watched him for a few minutes, noting that he'd occasionally put down his pen and hug the person whose book he'd autographed. The positive energy around him reminded me of what I'd just experienced with my father a few moments before—whoever this man was, I wanted to meet him. So I bought a copy of *The Power of Intention* and joined the long line to wait my turn.

When Dr. Wayne Dyer took my book to sign, he gave me a big smile and asked, "How are you doing, sweetheart?"

"Oh, I'm doing very well, Dr. Wayne. I'm so happy to meet you."

"Wow, what kind of accent is that? Where are you from?"

"I am from Rwanda."

"Rwanda? No, really?"

I smiled. He seemed so eager to meet me and so genuinely interested in my country that I felt special.

"Have you heard about the genocide?" he continued.

"Oh, I've heard all about it," I assured him.

"What happened was just terrible. Did you see the movie *Hotel Rwanda?*"

"Yes, I've seen it. It served a good purpose; it made people more aware of what we went through."

"So, you were there?"

"Yes." I had to laugh—even though we were discussing the holocaust, I loved this man's enthusiasm.

"Are you Hutu or Tutsi?"

"I'm Tutsi."

"Oh . . . but how did you survive?"

I began telling Wayne what happened to me during the genocide, but people in the line were getting impatient. I told him I didn't want to hold him up.

"Wait!" he said as I started to leave. "You're laughing and smiling, but you went through such a horrible time. What's your secret?"

"Oh, it's no secret: God taught me how to forgive. It's hard not to have love in your heart when God takes away all the hatred."

"Wow," he repeated. After a moment he excitedly asked, "Have you ever thought about writing a book about this?"

"I, um . . . I've written a few things down. . . ." I didn't want to tell him I'd just finished my manuscript in case he thought I'd come in looking for a favor.

"You absolutely must tell your story—you have to tell people what you've been through. If you write a manuscript, I'll make sure it gets published."

I think I gulped, but I know I couldn't think of anything to say. Our conversation had lasted only a minute or two, and this stranger was offering to help publish the manuscript he didn't even know was sitting at home beside my Bible. Was God teasing me? My mind was buzzing.

"Skye!" Wayne called out for his beautiful daughter. "Please trade e-mail information with this young lady. We've got a lot to talk about with her!"

When I got home that night, I still couldn't believe what had happened. From the dust jacket on *The Power of Intention*, I discovered that Dr. Wayne was a famous motivational speaker and writer whose work had been enjoyed by millions and millions of people! I read that book in one sitting, and to my delight found that a lot of it seemed to be about the power of prayer. But even with so many signs from God, doubt crept into my thoughts. I looked at my manuscript and then at the e-mail address I had for Skye Dyer, and then I remembered how I'd often been accused of being incredibly naïve.

Oh, he's such a famous writer, I fretted, *why would he bother with my little story? He was probably trying to be polite. I'm sure he won't even remember me, so I'm not going to embarrass myself by bothering him or his nice daughter. If he meant what he said, he'll call me. . . . I'll just wait.*

How many times had God come through for me when I asked Him for something? How often had I seen miracles happen? Could I even count the number of times I'd told people that if they had faith the size of a mustard seed, they could move mountains? God had never let me down, yet doubt still found a way to worm its way into my mind. That night I went to bed quite certain that Wayne had forgotten about me the moment I'd walked away from his book signing. I thought I'd been proven right after weeks went by with no word from Skye or Wayne.

"Oh well, God, I guess you don't want the book just yet," I said. But God had no intention of waiting and He pushed me to contact Wayne, sending me recurring dreams about the time I was a child on the hill near my home where Jeanette and I planned to plant a circle of beautiful flowers to encourage the Virgin Mary to appear to us. But we didn't get around to planting the flowers, and Mary appeared to children in another Rwandan village. Those dreams reminded me that, after the incident with the flowers and Mother Mary, I'd vowed to always follow through on my prayers and not just sit around waiting for God to drop what I'd asked for into my lap—I had to put my faith into action. I decided I would send Skye an e-mail, thanking her for being so sweet to me and to thank her father for his kind words. I pressed the send button on my work computer at the UN, even though I was positive by now that I was a long-forgotten memory in Wayne's active mind and busy life.

If my faith had wavered a little, Wayne's hadn't. It turned out I had misspelled my e-mail address when I gave it to Skye, who, at her dad's constant urging, had been repeatedly trying to contact me. Less than an hour after e-mailing Skye, I received a call on the phone at the UN.

I recognized Wayne's voice immediately. The first thing he said was, "You didn't call me back!"

"Oh, Dr. Wayne, I can't believe it's you! I didn't want to bother you. You are too busy to bother with someone like me."

"Immaculée, would you be willing to write down the story of how you survived the genocide? I feel I'm supposed to help you bring your story to the world."

My heart flipped.

"Well, to tell you the truth, Dr. Wayne, I've already written down most of what happened, but my English isn't very good, there are a lot of spelling mistakes, and I don't think people would be that interested . . ." I trailed off.

"Immaculée, listen to me. Your book is going to be a *New York Times* bestseller. Your message is going to reach the world."

"But you haven't even read it yet!"

"I don't have to read it . . . I can hear your story in your voice. If you can keep such joy after what you've been through—if you can still talk about God after seeing what you've seen—then this book is going to touch people. Your parents have reached down from heaven to help you tell this story, Immaculée, and God left you alive for a reason. Your tears are going to heal wounds, and your story is going to reach the world, believe me."

No one has ever told me anything that gave me more hope, more courage, and more faith in myself than what Wayne Dyer said during that short phone conversation. His words moved my heart, and his friendship changed my life. He did as he promised and took my manuscript to his publisher, Hay House. A little more than a year later, *Left to Tell* was in bookstores; and a few short weeks after that, it became a *New York Times* bestseller, just as Wayne predicted. Before I knew it, my book was being translated into 15 languages, and I was being asked to speak about God's power of forgiveness all over the world.

Wayne was right in that my story touched people, but it wasn't because it was *mine*. The story of Rwanda is one that belongs to us all. We don't have to experience genocide to know the darkness in which murder is born. Hatred, anger, mistrust, and fear enter our lives every day in a thousand different ways. We're all wounded by these evils, but we can all be healed through the power of love and forgiveness—a power readily available to all of us when we have faith. That was my message in *Left to Tell*, and I believe that this message is what resonated with so many.

Faith is a living thing that must be nurtured every day through prayer, kindness, and acts of love. It will lead us through our darkest days and restore love and light to even the most troubled soul in the most dire of circumstances. The power of God's forgiveness has even taken root again in my country: faith is flourishing where once there was only hatred and death. God's love is truly working a miracle in Rwanda.

Faith has transformed my life, and it can transform yours. In fact, it is powerful enough to transform the entire world.

EPILOGUE

Rwanda Rising

At the end of 2004, ten years after the genocide, and six years after I'd left for America, I returned to my homeland to attend my brother's wedding. It was a few weeks before Christmas, and I felt as if God had wrapped up Rwanda and handed it to me like an unexpected gift. From the moment I stepped off the plane in Kigali, I could feel a change in the air. My country was beautiful again.

The crumbling, broken wreck of a city I'd lived in after the genocide was nowhere to be found. A new Kigali had emerged from the ruins—one that was now bright, modern, inviting, and glistening in the morning sun. It was like arriving in a new world with a new family, which Bryan and I had added to by giving Nikki a wonderful brother, Bryan, Jr. (whom we affectionately call "B.J.").

Aimable picked the four of us up from the airport with his beautiful fiancée, Sauda. Like all of us, Sauda, a Tutsi, was putting tragedy behind her. She had been 18 when the killers had burst into her home and shot her family. She'd been grazed by a bullet and left for dead; but her parents, brothers, sisters, nieces, and nephews had all been killed.

When Sauda regained consciousness after the massacre, there was only one other person alive: her 16-year-old sister, Madeline, who had been shot in the chest. Sauda dragged her only remaining family member to an abandoned schoolhouse and held her

195

in her arms all night. "Don't let me die . . . I don't want to die," Madeline moaned, as she lay bleeding in Sauda's lap.

"I'm with you, Madeline," Sauda whispered. "Don't leave me alone; I won't survive without you." Her sister smiled up at her and then died in her arms.

Now Sauda was sitting in the front seat of my brother's car with her hand in his, two weeks away from their wedding and a future she'd thought she would never have. She lived with pain, but she also lived with hope. She had faith that God would make each day better than the last, and that was the beginning of happiness.

We drove through my old neighborhood, but I didn't recognize it. What had been a wasteland of charred rubble and scattered human bones was now a thriving suburb boasting hundreds of new family homes, complete with front yards filled with laughing children.

"Baby boom," Aimable remarked, smiling at Sauda. "There have been so many births in the last year that they're building new maternity clinics."

My brother had graduated with the highest marks for his year of any doctorate student in the country of Senegal. When he moved to Kigali, he'd spent a few tough years trying to get by, but he'd slowly established a good veterinary practice. He and Sauda planned to begin a family a year or two after their wedding.

"Look over there," he told us now, pointing to a small park where a dozen young parents were pushing youngsters on a large swing set. "It's the first-ever playground in Kigali! And they're about to start construction on the first public library in Rwanda as well."

We drove downtown, where rows of freshly planted saplings lined the roads. Wooden planters filled with flowers decorated the main intersections, which had formerly been military checkpoints topped by barbed wire. I noted that the streets were cleaner than any city I'd seen in either Africa or North America.

"We just had our monthly civic-cleanup day," Aimable explained. "A few weeks ago the government passed a law to keep

Kigali clean. They banned the use of plastic bags because they were cluttering up the city, and everybody had to take a day off work to pick up garbage. You should have seen it, Immaculée! Doctors, teachers, farmers, taxi drivers . . . everybody was out in the streets working together, trying to make the country beautiful! Everything is changing," he said excitedly.

My brother had always been a very stoic and reserved person—when we were growing up, convincing him to say more than "Good morning" was a daily family project. But the changes happening in the country had clearly energized every Rwandan; everyone was bursting with a pride they seemed compelled to share.

"And remember how hard it was to get into a good school?" Aimable asked me. When I nodded, he proudly announced, "Well, the government is building new universities all over the country. And there are many more grade schools, the literacy rate is jumping . . . so is the economy. People are working again. Oh, and you'd be happy to know that in the last national election, half of the politicians elected were women. You should move back to Rwanda and run for parliament!

"Do you know that women won almost 50 percent of the seats in the lower house of parliament? Think of it, Immaculée—50 percent! That means that tiny little Rwanda is leading all the other countries in the world for the number of women elected to parliament! We're making history!" my brother shouted excitedly, straining his neck to look back at me, his face beaming with pride.

"For heaven's sake, keep your eyes on the road, Aimable!"

I was proud of the progress women were making in Rwanda, and of my country itself. But, as I pointed out to my brother, "Who knows . . . maybe I will move back one day, but I would never, ever run for parliament. Leave that work for politicians; I'm only interested in doing God's work. Besides, I think the country is being run beautifully."

Paul Kagame was officially elected president in the 2000 elections, and he was doing an outstanding job. I remembered how all of us Tutsis had pinned our hopes on him and his rebel army to end the genocide. And he did—he'd driven off or destroyed the Interahamwe killers and ended the threat of insurgency. Many former Hutu soldiers had been peacefully repatriated, and the military presence in Kigali was more a symbol of peace and security than a reminder of war. The official government policy was for reconciliation, not revenge. As we drove through the beautiful new neighborhoods, I blessed President Kagame for he what he had made of the magnificent victory God had given him.

Unfortunately, while there had been more than 6,000 genocide trials in Rwanda, more than 100,000 Hutus were still in prison awaiting trial. The numbers were so great that they threatened to cripple the court system and drag out the prosecutions for generations, so the government reinstated a traditional system of justice called "gacaca." *Gacaca* means "on the grass," which describes the proceedings of the community courts that are held in outdoor clearings near the villages. The accused killers are brought to their communities to face their victims or their victims' families.

I could never bring myself to go to a gacaca, but my aunts found them therapeutic and went to several a month. As Jeanne explained, "I need to hear the details, Immaculée. I need to know how my children were killed so I can stop wondering and put it behind me. And I have to hear the killers apologize.

"It's a good form of justice," she insisted, "and it's justice the victims hand out ourselves. If the people at the gacaca don't believe what the killer says, or if we don't think his apology is sincere, we send him back to jail. If he convinces us that he is sincere, then we'll let him come back home. The worst criminals still have to go to court, and the organizers go to the international court . . . but our neighbors who picked up machetes have to answer to us."

I VISITED MANY OF MY OLD FRIENDS OVER THE NEXT TWO WEEKS. When I dropped by the Christus Center to say a prayer in the little room that had brought me so much solace, I ran into my cousin Ganza, now a full-time student of the Jesuit order. We sat in the same garden where years before we'd talked about the importance of Rwanda's new generation of clergy to rebuild the country's faith.

"It's happening," my cousin promised me. "It's happening right across the country. I never thought I would see it, but God is performing a miracle of forgiveness. Tutsis and Hutus are working together, volunteering their time and money to build new chapels and churches. Protestant, Catholic, Baptist, Episcopalian . . . people are embracing God from every denomination. Church attendance is higher than it's been in years. Christ has come to Rwanda, and there is joy in people's hearts. You can hear it in their voices when they sing on Sunday morning. You can hear the Holy Spirit in their songs!"

He smiled and added, "You were right, Immaculée—everything does begin with forgiveness. People are being open with each other and talking with less anger and suspicion about what happened. Killers return from jail and apologize to their victims, they beg to be forgiven. And I've often witnessed that forgiveness being granted. It will take a long time, but people *are* healing."

As always, the children at Mother Teresa's filled my heart with their warmth and love. After six years, many of the boys and girls I'd known were gone and new ones had taken their place, but the feelings were the same. Aimable, Nikki, and B.J. came with me for the visit, and we brought enough food and drinks to satisfy 200 big appetites. Our Christmas party continued until all of the orphans had gone to bed carrying a toy they'd selected from a big treasure box we'd hauled with us from America.

My own kids were able to see my childhood home in Mataba, along with the view of Lake Kivu that I'd grown up with. B.J. and Nikki were too young to understand why I was crying as I knelt by the graves of their grandmother and uncle, but they knew my tears were happy ones. My family in heaven was watching over my family on Earth.

Finally, I took my son and daughter to meet Pastor Murinzi. I hadn't seen him since he'd asked me to leave his house six years before, but when he saw me coming up his walk, he burst into tears.

"Daughter!" he cried out. After looking at Nikki and B.J., he whispered, "Daughter *and* mother." We hugged, and all was forgiven. While the pastor entertained the children, I went into the bathroom that had been my hiding place ten years earlier. I stood there alone, closed the door, shut my eyes, and thanked God for everything in my life.

THERE WERE MORE THAN 500 PEOPLE AT MY BROTHER'S WEDDING. Our spirits were so happy and light that I was sure Mom, Dad, Damascene, and Vianney had slipped in unnoticed and whispered blessings into our hearts.

The party went on well into the evening, and at one point I found myself standing on a hill at sunset looking over Kigali, as I had so many times over the years. Cousin Ganza had told me that people were healing in Rwanda, that faith was being restored. God, he said, was working a miracle of forgiveness in our country. Gazing out over the glowing city below me, I knew that this miracle would inspire the entire world. If the evil that was unleashed here could be conquered with love, where could evil not be conquered? If the hearts of Rwanda could be healed through forgiveness, then what heart couldn't?

The sun slipped beyond the horizon, its last rays illuminating the tops of a thousand hills. It was enough light for the entire world to see Rwanda rising from the ashes of genocide.

ACKNOWLEDGMENTS

First and foremost, I must thank God Almighty for all of His blessings. What did I do to deserve to be called Your child and be loved by You? I love You in return, with all the capacity to love that I possess.

To the Blessed Mother, I will thank you forever for coming to warn us in Kibeho. Although we didn't listen, you assured us that your son, Jesus, would love us anyway.

To my wonderful co-writer, Steve Erwin, thank you for sharing my pain and for lending me words to express my heart—first in *Left to Tell* and now in *Led by Faith*. My gratitude also goes to your wonderful and supportive wife, Natasha.

To Reid Tracy, president and CEO of Hay House, thank you for your faith, integrity, and constant support, as well as for finding an audience for my books. My gratitude also goes to Jill Kramer and the rest of your dedicated staff, who have worked so tirelessly on them.

To Suze Orman and Christiane Northrup, thank you both for leading the way for so many women and for all the love and support you have given me. I am forever grateful for all your help.

To Rick Warren, thank you for your encouragement and faith, and for the good works you do in Rwanda and around the world.

Many blessings to Amy Polaski for your deep faith; true friendship; and your dedicated fight to always bring more love, peace, and goodness to the world.

Thank you to my good friend Tim Van Damm, both for supporting this mission and *Our Lady of Kibeho.*

To all my friends and family who supported me with love, and in so many different ways gave me the courage to finish this book, God bless you all—I love each and every one of you.

And finally, thanks to the people of Rwanda, whose courage, willingness to forgive, and faith in God continues to inspire me and will soon inspire the entire world.

— Immaculée

❖ ❖

Immaculée, thank you for your continued trust in me to write your inspiring story. Your love of God and faith in human goodness has touched my heart; you enrich all our lives.

Many, many thanks to Jill Kramer at Hay House for your unfailing professionalism and unflagging patience. Many thanks as well to Reid Tracy, Shannon Littrell, Christy Salinas, Stacey Smith, and all the other fine folks at Hay House.

To Faith Farthing of FinalEyes Communications, thank you for your keen-eyed observations and exacting attention to detail.

My heart and everything in it goes to my beautiful and talented wife, Natasha Stoynoff, whose smile never fails to light up my life, make me laugh, and lift my spirit—thank you for it all. And to you, Tatko, thanks for all the perfectly steeped Dell Park teas, teaching me to love Dickens, and how to avoid a right jab. A special, heartfelt note of thanks to my parents, Isobel and Jim, for the lifetime of love and support you've given me. And, of course, thank you to my loving and beloved sister, Dr. Lorna Erwin; and my three great brothers, Blake, Doug, and Big Davey.

And finally, my deepest thanks to Stephen Longstaff. You are my brother in both law and in life—my teacher; my mentor; and my dear, dear friend.

— **Steve Erwin**

❖ ❖

ABOUT THE AUTHORS

Immaculée Ilibagiza was born in Rwanda and studied electronic and mechanical engineering at the National University. She lost most of her family during the 1994 genocide. Four years later, she emigrated to the United States and soon began working at the United Nations in New York City. She is now a full-time public speaker and writer. In 2007 she established the Left to Tell Charitable Fund, which helps support Rwandan orphans.

Immaculée holds honorary doctoral degrees from the University of Notre Dame and St. John's University, and was awarded the Mahatma Gandhi International Award for Reconciliation and Peace 2007. She is the author, with Steve Erwin, of *Left to Tell: Discovering God Amidst the Rwandan Holocaust.*

Steve Erwin is a Toronto-born writer and award-winning journalist working in the print and broadcast media. Most recently, he was the New York foreign correspondent for the Canadian Broadcasting Corporation. He co-authored the *New York Times* bestselling memoir *Left to Tell.* He lives in Manhattan with his wife, journalist and author Natasha Stoynoff.

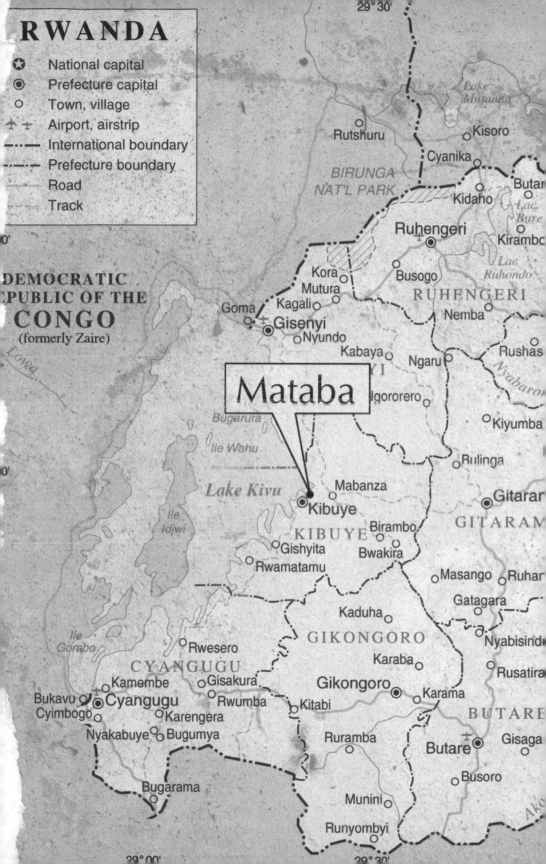